FROM HELL TO HEALING

Relentless Pursuit

Elizabeth DeBerry

Copyright © 2023 by Elizabeth DeBerry
All rights reserved.

ISBN: 979-8-218-26023-1

SPECIAL THANKS

Shout out to Restored Hope Ministries! Pastors Sam and Sherry and all of the selfless volunteers - thank you for seeing, loving, and accepting me just the way I came into the program, and then, for refusing to let me stay in that condition.

Mom and Dad - I don't even have the words. ♥ May God abundantly give you back everything you have so graciously poured into my life, and then some.

Mom and Dad DeBerry - God knew exactly what he was doing! You two together are like the glue that will hold the generations coming behind you, together, challenging them to follow in your footsteps for years to come. Keep serving the King 👑 and greater still will be your reward! Thank you for accepting me into your family!

To my little Sis - I love you! I am so sorry for everything I have done. I hope one day you will find it in your heart to forgive me. I miss you, dear sister. ♡ 🩹

To my sister Erin - You are the definition of JOY! I wish I had a million balloons and mirrors to give you! But don't worry, Heaven will handle that one day, I'm sure of it! 😆

To the rest of the Godings, Andersons, and DeBerrys - thank you for all your support, love, and much-needed prayers. You are warriors, and I couldn't do any of this without you.

Dearest Jane - thank you for listening to me read these devotionals for hours on end. You are a true friend and blessing from God.

Maggie and Mario - you have been such an inspiration and an example in my life. You two are an amazing example of what God designed marriage to become. I cherish you both.

Alicia and Steve - thank you for investing in our marriage! We are so blessed to have you in our lives! May God continue to strengthen your gifts as you so graciously impart them to others.

To my husband - every time I look at you, I see the faithfulness of God and His promises spoken over my life. You are truly my special Gift from God and answer to many prayers. Thank you for your integrity, support, and kindness! Thank you for being my #1 cheerleader!!! 📣 Thank you for all the time and words of encouragement you have poured into this book. These pages would still be collecting dust in a closet somewhere if it hadn't been for your consistent motivation! I love you more than words can express. May God continue to uphold you with his righteous right hand - and shower you with blessings!

RELENTLESS PURSUIT

Dedicated to Restored Hope Ministries

She had a name once...
and it wasn't given to her as a result of her bad decisions;
she was loved...
Long before time existed, Heaven had already called her
Long before her parents had even given her a thought,
she was already a twinkle in the eyes of God.
Sometime, somewhere... she was Daddy's little girl.
She was marked.

And although Heaven holds her true identity
she still answers to the names the world has called her
and now she wears another name.

In a reckless attempt to relieve her shame
she grasped for freedom from a source that
would ultimately detain her.

She's now gone missing,
an unidentified little girl is now trapped inside
her own invisible prison.

We must find her!
We must be willing to lay down our labels, leave the 99...
Go into the darkness, risking it all to bring her back.
She still has her true name.
She still has a purpose.
And... she is still Daddy's little girl.

Jesus gave His life to save her... and you... and me.
We must be willing to do the same.

Join us in His Relentless Pursuit

MY TESTIMONY

From Hell to Healing ♡ 🩹

The rope tightened around my neck; I couldn't breathe. As I went in and out of consciousness, all I can remember thinking is, "This is it; I'm about to die." And then it hit me; a wave of sadness stronger than words. My life was being taken, breath by breath, by a demon-possessed drug addict. I saw the darkness creep across his eyes just moments before the decision was made to kill me. He wasn't alone, but then again, neither was I.

The overwhelming sadness just moments before my death came from being full; I was full of grief, I was full of remorse, but I was also full of purpose! This book that you are about to read almost ended up in the graveyard.

As a young teenager, I ran away from home to Miami, Florida. I was there just under a week before I was kidnapped by sex traffickers. I knew I had encountered this demon before, but back then he had many different faces. One by one, they came down to my room and raped me, each one taking with them a piece of my soul until one day, I too had become the darkness.

By God's grace, I eventually escaped, but I was never free. Shackled to shame, my soul tied to the lies the monsters had left behind: unworthy, broken, and stained. These are just a handful of names that began replacing my own. I was dead inside the walls of my own identity, and the monsters I'd been running from reappeared every time I caught my reflection in the mirror.

I was becoming one with the darkness. The flicker of hope, the only light left within my eyes, now glossed over with every heroin high. I had renounced my crown and taken up the needle; the position I now held, no greater than just another beggar in the street.

I went from being a beloved daughter to becoming dangerous and deceived. I wasted years here, and I was about to die here. My life replayed itself like a horror movie. My role as both the victim and the villain flashed before my eyes as tears flowed to the floor. For the first time in my life, I could see clearly. The hope buried deep within my soul began to rise up. I wasn't alone either, and I refused to die in this condition.

My father used to tell me as a young child, "Remember who you are." With the noose still wrapped tightly around my neck I began to pray. At that moment, I remembered! Like a fountain well springing up in the deserted wastelands of my soul flowed the buried memories of Sunday school, family devotions, and praying grandparents. It is well; it is well with my soul.

The old Baptist hymns I'd been forced to sing as a kid jumped off their dusty pages and landed in my mouth; I remembered! Sobered up for only a moment, my eyes lit up once again from a smoldering fire buried deep within my bones. This was a moment of redemption, a second chance to do just one thing in my life worth dying for. My soul stood up. Fear gave way to faith as I began speaking to the little boy buried deep beneath the demonic mask.

 "I forgive you; I forgive you; I forgive you…
Jesus loves you; Jesus loves you; He loves you!
Jesus, I'm begging you to please have mercy on this man. Forgive him, please because he knows not what he does. Show him how much you love him, Jesus. Help him to know

you, Jesus. I do not hold anything he has done against him" - the words released just above the sound of a whisper prayed through tears.

"Please don't stop praying!" the demon-possessed man cried out as he dropped to his knees; a single tear managed to escape the darkness of his cold eyes as it rolled down his cheek and hit the floor. I remembered that I too was not alone.

I reached back to a place outside the realm of time and grabbed hold of a combined strength from all the saints that had gone before me. I rose boldly to my feet, covered by the blood and with the full force of heaven's army behind me, and I spoke, this time directly to the demon.

"In the name of Jesus - LEAVE!!!!"

In an instant, the darkness was gone. I held the sobbing, attempted murderer for a just moment longer, reminding him, once again, that he was forgiven before unlocking the door and running for my life.

This demonic encounter was the first tangible seed of healing planted along my journey. It marked me. It changed me. Jesus was in a relentless pursuit of my heart, and He adamantly refused to let me go.

Several months later, I miraculously landed at Restored Hope Ministries in Dallas, a Safe House for women whose lives have been adversely affected by Sex Trafficking, drugs, and homelessness. I was still a long way off from being free, but I was safe, I was loved, and I was seen.

I began writing, nearly seven years ago, at the beginning of my healing journey. It's been more valleys than hills, but climbing, nonetheless. In no way, shape, or form do I claim to have it all together, or to have everything figured out just yet... But I'm still here, I'm still standing, and I'm so very grateful to be alive! Packed between these pages, you will find the treasure of pain that's finally found its purpose.

So, cheers to everyone who is graciously reading this book. I believe in you! I believe in your healing and more importantly, God believes in you! I'm right here with you as you embark on this beautiful journey toward wholeness. We all are in this fight together!

Let's remember who we are!!!

All my love,

Beth

FROM THE ASHES

Up from the ashes she arose
Bearing scars, with soot-stained feet.
Broken-winged little girl
Yet refusing to accept defeat.
As demons stole her innocence
Bars of shame became her cell
Haunted by past memories
She had made her bed in Hell.
The devil thought he had her
He thought she was his lover
But she belonged to someone else
A Lover like no other!
He came with keys and paid the price
His life, to set her free
Unable to fly with broken wings
So, love came down to me.
In the fires of Hell, Love took my hand and raised me to my feet
Broken-winged little girl, get up, it's time for you to eat!
The tables prepared, with the 99 there, left behind I came down just for you
And I'd do it again, to see broken wings mend, there is nothing my Love will not do!
So, up from the ashes she arose
Bearing scars and soot-stained feet
With mended wings, she took to the sky
And at the table, she found her seat!
Broken-winged little girl, redeemed by her true Lover
From now until the end of time, there will never be another!

WOUNDS AND SCARS

A wound is painful. If not treated properly, it can get infected and eventually, in some cases, may even lead to death. Some wounds, such as nicks, scrapes, and paper cuts tend to heal rather quickly, while others like burns, for instance, can take months or even years to heal properly. Even then, the process of healing is excruciatingly painful! Scars are the marks left behind after the healing process. Depending on the severity of the wound, some scars are more prevalent than others.

A wise person once told me, the difference between a wound and a scar is simply the presence of pain at the point of pressure. If I put my finger on it, does it still hurt? Scabs and band-aids can cover a wound, but they cannot manufacture the time and treatment needed to heal what's festering underneath the surface. Isn't this the same principle spiritually? How do I know if I'm healed? I've learned to ask myself, "Does this still cause pain when someone brings it up? Or can I talk openly about what happened?" The cuts, scrapes, wounds, and burns of this life will always leave a mark. Some, you can plainly see, while others you would have to point out to notice they exist. Sometimes, God puts his finger on something I thought was a scar, and with his heavenly hands, gently holding the makeshift bandage I patched together out of denial, doubt, and shame, he lovingly asks me with care, compassion, and love of a good father, "Are you ready to deal with this?" Ripping off the band-aid is going to hurt like hell, and the pain of the process to follow will probably bring me to my knees. But deep down I know it's for my good, and if I don't deal with the infection festering underneath, eventually it will spread to my bloodstream and my entire being will become infected.

Hurt people hurt people whether they intended to or not! The healing finger of God is always after our open wounds. He wants to make your test a testimony, your mess a message, and your scars the platform on which the story of his amazing Grace is preached and proclaimed. Will you let him? He won't start the healing process without your permission! Trust the process. People are waiting on the power of your healing testimony!

Psalm 147:3: "He heals the brokenhearted and binds up the wounds."

Challenge: Where are your soul wounds? What area still causes pain at the point of pressure?

Prayer: God, healing often hurts, but I trust you. I trust your scars as proof that healing is possible. I give you permission to remove my band-aids. Hold my hand through this hell. Bind up my insecurities so that my pain will not reproduce itself in others. Let me boldly wear my scars, like you, as a testimony of your amazing grace.

A FAULTY FOUNDATION

Skylines worldwide are the canvas for some of the most amazing and breathtaking architectural sights known to mankind. These monstrous monuments can be seen for miles and miles, and some can even be spotted from clear across the sea. Towers of steel and glass are carefully constructed and uniquely designed to captivate our attention and serve the industrial delights of forward revolution. When gazing upon these breathtaking beauties one can't help but stare in awe and wonder at their majestic strength becoming ever so humbled as our awareness of our weakness gives birth beneath their shadows. Designed to withstand hurricane-force winds, earthquakes, and other natural elements, these evolutionary structures stand out and boldly announce their presence.

What we see with the naked eye when captivated by these spectacular skylines is a direct result of what we don't. These buildings, as strong and glorious as they appear, have no hope of holding up themselves. In essence, they are all really only as strong as the foundation they stand upon. A faulty foundation, no matter how strong, purposed and carefully crafted the building, will one day be the cause of its demise bringing destruction to everyone and everything it's connected to.

We, as believers, are called to a life of construction. We have been designed and purposed to build, but before we go up we must be willing to go down, dig deep, and fully focus on our foundations. When we choose to build on half-truths and partial healing, our best presentations to the world will become like that of the fool who chose to build his house upon the sand. It may look strong, breathtaking, and glorious on the outside - the external, but given the perfect set of circumstances, we are only one storm or trial away from mass destruction. It is the unseen cement of preparation, prayer, obedience, and a prostrate heart before God that seals the cracks and fortifies our foundations. If we forsake the darkroom of development or bypass the pruning process of sanctification, we will structure our lives on top of a platform that will not be able to sustain the weight of its purpose. When we build before we've been built, and when we fall (and we will), we will inevitably take others down in our demise.

Yes, we are called and commissioned, but are we approved? The high calling and construction of Christ demand a constant state of internal foundational inspection. To build His Kingdom, we first must be willing and allow him to demolish our own. Let's be like the wise man who built his house upon the Rock, so when the rain comes down and the floods come up what was built up in and on Christ will last forever!

Matthew 7: 24-27: "Therefore everyone who hears these words of mine and puts them into practice is like a wise man who built his house on the rock. The rain came down, the streams rose, and the winds blew and beat against that house; yet it did not fall, because it had its foundation on the rock. But everyone who hears these words of mine and does not put them into practice is like a foolish man who built his house on sand. The rain came down, the streams rose, and the winds blew and beat against that house, and it fell with a great crash."

Challenge: Where is your foundation? What man-made kingdoms have you been building?

Prayer: Father, show me the gaps in my foundation. I give you permission to tear down any dream or vision I've built without you. Help me fix the places I don't often see as broken. Help me build your unshakeable kingdom. In Jesus name-Amen.

TANGLED IN TOXICITY

Therefore, since we are surrounded by such a great cloud of witnesses, let us throw off everything that hinders and the sin that so easily entangles (**Hebrews 12:1**).

We all have vices. Those things and people we run to when we get thirsty. Depletion is dangerous, and if we don't learn to discern our drought; we will chase after counterfeit rain, wetting our palates temporarily, but never fully able to saturate our souls. For some of us, the entanglement in toxicity is obvious. We have a full-blown love affair with a pornographic website, have a pipe or pill in our mouth, or a needle in our vein. For others, the dance with the devil is much more discreet. From entertaining affirmations through our DMs to an extra scoop of ice cream when we are feeling rejected or devalued. It's easy to label the latter as less consequential but hidden has never equated to being less harmful; as a matter of fact, the exact opposite is true.

When we engage in extravagant, blasphemous behavior, we are well aware of the consequences ahead of time. We don't need a PH.D. or an extremely high spiritual IQ to understand that 2+2 always equals 4. Gambling always equals debt, addiction always equals burned bridges and loss, and homosexuality and pornography always equals bondage and perversion. We know this! We are fully aware of the warning labels on these toxic chemicals before ingestion. Even those unable to read can see the skull and crossbones on the bottle.

We partake in these behaviors and relationships by choice. It's rebellion; it's intentional; it's highly toxic, and in the end, will always lead to death. But what about the smaller "sins"? The ones that come with far less judgment, if any at all? What about our casual commitments to our Facebook friends, with benefits that stroke our egos and feed our fallenness? What about our extra drink to numb the pain in pursuit of peace of mind? What about a shopping spree birthed from a place of lack or discontentment? What about feeding our thirst with a Netflix series instead of our spirits with the truth and water of the word?

These are the entanglements in toxicity that are far less easily discerned, but equally if not entirely more dangerous. These are the silent killers of our secrets. The slow fade, the smart thieves that rob us one treasure at a time, so that we are unaware of anything being missing or out of place until it's entirely too late. It's the extra cupcake once a day that two years later, leads to obesity. It's the casual, barely crossing-the-line instant messaging that months later turns into a fully-fledged emotional affair, robbing us of our real relationships. It's the distracting and perverted thoughts that we refuse to cast out and allow to live rent-free in our heads. Over time, they inhabit so much of our headspace, it becomes impossible to discern their lies from His truth.

These are the leeches of liability that suck the spiritual life out of us, one drop at a time. We can see from a distance these leper-like toxic sin infections. Their own lifestyle choices always scream out, "Unclean!" We can even look at our leprosy in the mirror, and the reflection is always undistorted and the same. We are sick. We can see it, and so can everyone else who is closely connected to us. But what about the hidden virus of COVID- like sin toxicity? The one that lives long before we ever see its symptoms? The one that is mass infecting others due to a lack of self-awareness of its infection? As carriers, we can gaze into the same mirror completely unaware that the reflection we are seeing is a distorted and counterfeit view of ourselves. We are functional. We look healthy and no one around us knows we are sick, including ourselves. This is the entanglement in toxicity that is far more dangerous. Everything and everyone we touch is now at risk. And we don't come with a warning label. There is nothing about our secret sins that scream out, "Unclean!" But long after we have left, the seed born out of our thirst remains, still steals, and still silently kills.

Everything that we do both affects or infects ourselves and others, even when we are completely unaware of its toxicity. The enemy always is, and always has been after our hearts because out of our hearts flows all things! He knows just how to take out the body of Christ with COVID-like sin toxicity. He is the author and architect of mass genocide, and he comes in one thought, one message, and one extra cupcake at a time. We must learn to discern his tactical blueprints of death. When we have been released from the prison of our leper-like toxic rebellion, it's easy to then strut our new identities down the catwalk of religion and somehow think we have attained a higher level of spirituality. We then start living out our COVID-like toxic freedom, infecting everyone around us, yet completely unaware of the damage and destruction we are still capable of causing.

What are we carrying around without symptoms? What types of Hell are we harboring in our hearts? What demonic tenants in our minds do we have that need to be served an eviction notice, or DM respondents that need to be deleted without an explanation? It's the secret sins, the slow fade, and the silent killers that need to be discerned and put to death. It's the pet tigers (sin) in our backyards that we keep feeding and loving. One day, we will step outside just like all the other days to feed, pet, and play with it, and eventually, it will eat us, or someone else we dearly love, alive.

Genesis 4:7: Sin is crouching at the door eager to control you. But you must subdue it and be its master."

Challenge: What pet tigers (sin) are you feeding, loving, and playing around with? What/who in your life needs to be met with an exit strategy or symbolic execution?

Prayer: Heavenly Father, I acknowledge that sometimes I pet and play with my sin instead of destroying it. Give me the strength to destroy my sin before it destroys me. Show me the people, and vices from which I need to walk away. I know I can't do it without the power of the Holy Spirit. In Jesus' name, Amen.

INDEPENDENCE

I've searched high and low for independence. I've crossed state lines, personal boundaries, and legal limits, all for the sake of freedom. I've chased feelings, impulses, and even demons in disguise, but the morning after, I remained locked behind the bars of my bad decisions. Freedom, to me, was always fleeting, but maybe that's because I had confused freedom with escape. My whole life I've been in a perpetual state of running, but usually the thing I'm running from isn't nearly as reckless and raunchy as what I'm running to. I'm searching for rest, not in a place or a person, but in my soul. Inner peace has been the unspoken buried treasure of my quest for independence.

But my resources are running ragged, and my perseverance tank showed empty, two miles ago. I'm running out of motivation and inspiration. I've been desperate for so long that I'm growing accustomed to these chains. Rather than change, I may just continue to manage my condition. I'm functionally uncomfortable, but not to the point of the pressure that demands change. I've outlasted my unmet expectations and re-lived nightmares, as I've watched my dreams slowly die off, one by one.

But I'm still here because I'm resilient. Some might call it stupid; others might call it something much worse, but when your best friend is Failure, names don't matter much anymore. Tick-Tock, I'm running out of time, breathing to death in a broken system and an invisible prison. What do you do when your only chance of freedom is escape, and the one thing you can't escape from is yourself?

My quest for independence is going to kill me. Maybe that's been the point from the beginning. I decrease so that He increases. I die to myself so He can live through me.

The funny thing is, I've been searching high and low for independence, and it was right here in me the whole time.

Independence, like most things we search for, cannot be found. We must give it up. Just as the seed falls to the ground, is buried, and dies, so must our quest for independence die. Only then can our true self be raised. As we walk in obedience and let go of control, we begin to bear fruit, not for ourselves, but for Him who set us free.

Freedom is much less a destination than it is a decision. I die daily.

I lay it down so that He can lift it up. Independence is not a date, or a place, it is a name.

Freedom has a face.

His name is Wonderful Counselor, Prince of Peace, Almighty God, the Alpha and the Omega, the Beginning, and the End, the First and the Last, the Word, the Well, and the Water within.

Jesus Christ! Independence is my dependence; freedom is my foundation.
He is, He was, and He always will be. **I am!!!**

Mark 8:34-35: "If anyone wishes to come after me, let him deny himself, and take up his cross, and follow me, for whoever wishes to save his life shall lose it; but whoever loses his life for my sake and the gospel's, shall save it."

Challenge: Where have you searched for independence outside of Christ?
What was the result? What's one step towards freedom that you could take today?

Prayer: Jesus, in you alone am I free. Teach me how to die to my flesh. Daily. so that You can live and move through me freely. Thank You for my freedom! Amen

FIGHT OR FLIGHT

If running from problems was an Olympic event, I would hold several gold medals by now. Fight or flight is a real subconscious defense mechanism located in the part of your brain that acts first and thinks later (at least that's how I imagine it goes down in my mind.)

Since I was in grade school, I've kept a pair of track shoes and utilized them every time a situation would arise that was too painful or scary to face head-on. Conflict would approach, and my brain would press the red button activating my flight response. Before I even had time to process the situation, I was already off to the races.

As I grew in age, this habitual response became more and more dangerous. The things and people I was running to turned out to be far worse than the problems from which I was running. After a while, it dawned on me that I was running in circles. I was stuck in a perpetual cycle of escape, and in a circle, there is no exit strategy. It was insane! Like a hamster on a wheel, always running but never changing locations or moving forward.

God Himself had to interrupt my insanity. I was built to run, yes, but His path is towards purpose, not in a loop. Turns out, I can't run forward until I confront what's behind me, and within me. So, God made it His mission to confront my cowardice and turn it into confidence! As I've repented, he has turned my circles into open highways.

Fight or flight is a real response programmed into the foundation of who we are. God renewed my mind with the power of the blood of Jesus and taught me how to fight off the darkness and those things, places, and people prohibiting my flight. This hamster is no longer on a wheel, stuck in a loop. I'm still running, but now I'm running the race.

Verse: Hebrews 12:1: "Let us run with endurance the race set before us, looking to Jesus, the founder and perfecter of our faith, who for the joy set before him endured the cross, despising the shame, and is seated at the right hand of the throne of God."

Challenge: What loops, sin patterns, and cycles are you stuck running in? What people, places, or things are preventing you from reaching your purpose?

Prayer: God, help me to identify those sin patterns and strongholds that have kept me stuck in a loop. Always moving, but never taking new ground. I don't want to run away or in circles. Teach me how to confidently confront the enemy - the inner me. I want to run my race well. In Jesus' name, Amen!

RUNNING IN CIRCLES

I should have been a track star! If running away from problems was an Olympic event, I would have medals, stacked on medals, showcased next to trophies. If there's one thing I know how to do well, I know how to move! Forward movement resides deep within my DNA. I can move over, move out of the way, move around, back, or run up, but the one thing I don't know how to do, despite all my exhausted efforts, is to stand still.

Oh, trust me, I've tried, but the harder I try, the more out of sorts I become, and like a wild Mustang contained in a stall, I'll just end up kicking my way out, bucking and fighting against the very structure built to keep me safe. I'm constantly biting at the hand attempting to feed me, rebelling and resisting the very process that's meant to free me. The breaking process, events, interactions, and even distractions cumulated in such a significant sequence, that the once wild and untamed creature, is now re-programmed and aligned for the Master's use.

I fight against the goads because my pride refuses to bow down and humbly relinquish my false sense of security, stemming from my need to feel in control. But it's just an illusion. A misrepresentation and counterfeit existence to my reality. All my years of running, yet still no tangible progress accomplished. It's hard to be a hardwired visionary, built for forward movement while stuck in a loop, like a hamster spinning on a wheel. It's a broken cycle. The faces change, but the patterns remain all too familiar.

Surrendering is the key, unlocking the door called Freedom, but standing in front of it are demonic lies blocking and taunting my true identity. "If you let him break you, you will no longer be a wild horse. He will strip away the part that gives you heart, the part that's wild and free, and instead, you will be a slave by force, whipped into submission and beaten down until you no longer have a choice." But then speaks the other voice, no louder than a whisper, with a question I never did think before to ask myself. "Who told you that? Who is this unseen author of fear that's run you everywhere but here, into the arms of the only one in the world qualified to tame you? And yes, I do break you, but it's only to rebuild you; the world that has attempted to put you together has left many pieces broken and out of place. Daughter, lift your head. I've never beaten my children into submission. I don't call or treat them like slaves, I give them names! Adopted daughters and sons! Broken or wild, you will never lose your ability to choose, neither will I ever remove the gift I've given you to run! But if willingly submitted, I will turn your hamster loops into highways and resistance into roads of redemption and deliverance.

"If you stop running from me and learn to run toward me, I can teach you how to run with me and then together we will run right over the enemy en route to your destiny with an entirely resurrected identity! That is, if you trust me enough to remove you from your loop."

Challenge: In what hamster loops are you stuck running?

Prayer Time: Sit for a few minutes alone with God and ask Him to show you the areas where you keep going in circles.

RUNNING INTO WALLS

Opportunity is usually met head-on by opposition or resistance. Recently, I've been trying to make amends and rebuild relationships, a kind of deep cleanse or " bridge restoration," so to speak. When it came down to making amends with my father and restoration in our relationship, I felt like I just kept hitting a brick wall.

I remember sharing this in a group session during my time in rehab, when the Holy Spirit impressed on my spirit that if I continued to run into the same wall long enough, eventually, instead of bouncing off, I would ultimately breakthrough! Some of us have years and years of damage that we've caused, and despite our good intentions or moral motives, we are still seen through the colored lenses of our past mistakes and failures. Don't get me wrong, I'm not excusing unforgiveness. I'm just asking us to continue to give grace and continue to grab hold and seize every opportunity for restoration, even when it feels like we are running into walls.

Sometimes the only way people know how to protect themselves from pain is to build a self-made fortress around their hearts. Guarding our hearts is biblical! That fortress was laid brick by brick, disappointment by disappointment, unfulfilled promise by unfulfilled promise, lie after lie, and let down after let down. It's not going to crumble in a day's work. I believe a wrecking ball cannot only bring demolition and destruction, but breakthrough and deliverance, depending on the driving force behind the blow.

Keep running after restoration, keep pressing into progress, keep showing up in the face of opposition, and keep fighting back with grace. Eventually, the point of pain and the wall of resistance will become the hole of access, allowing God the space and freedom to do the work that only He can do. Keep running into walls!

2 Chronicles 5:18-20: "All this is from God, who reconciled us to himself through Christ and gave us the ministry of reconciliation that God was reconciling the world to himself in Christ, not counting people's sins against them. And he has committed to us the message of reconciliation. We are therefore Christ's ambassadors, as though God were making his appeal through us. We implore you on Christ's behalf: Be reconciled to God."

Challenge: Think about a relationship in your life that needs restoration/reconciliation.

Prayer Time: Sit alone with God and ask Him to show you what the next step toward reconciling that relationship looks like. Be willing to hear His response.

HELLS WELLS

All of humanity was born thirsty. It's the predispositional curse of our existence. The empty and innate spaces of our souls that scream and beg to be filled, but far too often settle for just a fix, like a dope fiend hole in our hearts, relentlessly searching, yet never full.

The woman at the well was well acquainted with this vampire-like drive beneath the surface layer of her identity. The bloodlust of our depravity perpetually hunts to feed the need. It's the unseen force of insanity, continually drawing us towards darkness, while whispering to the void. Hells Wells calls out to our deepest insecurities. They play on our need to feed and speak intimately to our emptiness. These are the demons dressed up as our distractions. The princes of counterfeit promises, the strippers of God's standards, and the cosigners of compromise. They are the death riders to our purpose and the gravediggers to our potential.

The tricks and tactics of the enemy remain the same today. He targets our thirst and caters to our soul caverns. He not only understands but has mastered our thirst trap, knowing just the right meal to make us move. Hells Wells won't kill us, but they will drown out what's been placed deep within us. They are the pits of stagnation, the holes of habitual sin, and the caves of temporary comfort. We are no different or better than the woman at the well. We are all drinking from somewhere other than the source.

Jesus spoke to her the same way he is speaking to each one of us now: "My Child, if you only knew the gift God has for you, and who you are speaking to, you would ask me, and I would give you living water." Until we fully believe He knows and wants what's best for us, we will continuously repeat the same cycles of insanity, albeit with different faces and new outfits, stuck in the same loop! To deny we are thirsty is to be deceived, and to attempt to feed ourselves is foolish.

John 4:10 "If you only knew the gift God has for you and who you are speaking to, you would ask me, and I would give you living water."

Challenge: What wells have you been running to outside of Jesus? What has been the result?

Prayer: God, You know, and I know that I'm thirsty! You designed the space that screams and begs to be filled! Teach me how to hunger and thirst after your righteousness! Make me aware of the counterfeit wells I'm drawing water from, attempting to meet and feed my own needs. Help me to remember and remind me over and over again, that you alone are enough! Give me this living water so that my life can become an overflowing well for others. In Jesus' name, Amen!

WORTHY OF IT ALL!

Make my life an altar, worthy of your fire,
Burn out my imperfections, purify my desire
Torch this heart and fan the flame,
Test me through and through
Idolatry to ashes, I want to look like You!
Confront my comfortable kingdoms,
Send your fire down,
Stand with me in the furnace,
Till I'm no longer bound
With Your match to all my motives I can freely love my brother
Your candle loses nothing when it's lighting up another
So, light me up, and burn me out
Smoke me through and through
Approve my life as incense, holy and pleasing to You
Make my life an altar, build your firewall
I give you all the glory
You're worthy of it all!

THE LENS OF LOSS

We have all experienced and are familiar with some kind of loss. For some of us, it was the death of a loved one, for others it was a relationship gone bad, or a friendship that fell off unexpectedly, but no matter the backstory, the internal struggle is real. Pain will always leave a mark, and if we are not careful, pain will then become the pen picked up and used to continue writing our stories.

Loss affects our souls and reaches the innermost chambers of our hearts. Loss leaves no one out in its quest for devastation and depression. Loss is relentless, weighty, and completely invasive. Loss, in the devil's hand, becomes a weapon, and loss yielded by Hell will rip us to pieces from the inside out. So, what do we do? How do we keep from being utterly destroyed by our pain? How can we walk through a heartbreaking process and still come out on the other side unbroken?

Pain without a purpose becomes poisonous, and when we allow loss to become our lens, everything we are connected to becomes infected. I know when pain is my pen, I assign, and I assume. I start writing my own opinions fueled by feelings and leave out any room for grace. My pain-filled perspective will usually point fingers, if not throw up the middle one, and then run backward toward things, patterns, and people from which I've already been delivered. I must learn to hand over my pen to God. He is the only source that can attach purpose to our pain. I must trust that He is both willing and capable to reposition my pain and write GLORY into my story.

It's not enough to KNOW; I must BELIEVE that what the enemy meant for evil, God will always turn into something for my good. That doesn't mean it feels good, and it doesn't mean I deny the pain exists. It just means that I allow God into the deepest parts of my soul and the innermost chambers of my broken heart, allowing Him to reconstruct the pieces. I let Him become the Author of my circumstances. Pain that should have broken me, ends up building me when God holds the pen. He is waiting to re-write your story too!

Romans 8:18: "Yet what we suffer now is nothing compared to the glory He will reveal to us later."

Challenge: In what ways have we allowed pain to become the pen used in writing our stories?

Prayer: God, the weight of loss is too heavy for me to carry. I've been resentful of You and others because I've mismanaged my pain. I know You have more for my life than this. I know you work all things together for my good even if I can't see it at the moment. Help me to relinquish control of my pain and hand the "pen" over to you, to continue working on your masterpiece. I trust you. In Jesus' name, Amen.

LETTING GO

It's crazy the way God gives us revelations sometimes! I learned a powerful lesson today from a little dog named Crumpet. Crumpet is a rescue dog. I don't know her full history, but usually, dogs that end up in rescues have less than a picture-perfect past.

Crumpet came to our hospital with a broken leg. It was broken beyond repair, but it didn't stop her sweet-spirited little heart one bit. She hobbled along and did the best she could, attempting to walk on a limb that no longer served its purpose. It was a part of her. With every step, it caused her great pain, but because it was the only way she knew how to walk, she winced, cried, and continued to use it, nonetheless. Every morning we came into work, and the staff was greeted by her wagging tail and kisses. I would have never known or guessed by the way she carried herself that she was injured. She was broken, but she had learned to live with the brokenness. Remember, she learned how to walk with all of those legs! They were a part of her! But now, something that used to help her was hindering and hurting her, but she couldn't imagine a life walking without it. If it was up to Crumpet, she would probably still be hobbling along with a broken leg, but because we knew something that she didn't, and because we wanted the best for her, we made the hard decision for her. We amputated it.

This was on Friday. I came to work Monday, half expecting to see Crumpet in the corner crying and moping over the loss of her much-loved leg, but to my surprise, her greeting was still the same! Full of excitement with a wagging tail and kisses! I took her for her morning walk. She stumbled along for a little bit, but after a few minutes, she was walking like a champ! She had a few faceplants, which I'm sure didn't feel great at the time, but once she figured it all out and learned how to walk all over again, she was then able to take steps without the leg that caused her pain.

There are things in each one of our lives that we have learned to walk with. Even good things that, at some point, no longer serve a purpose. Those are the things that are hardest to let go. They are things, patterns, and people, that at one point brought us life and joy, and may even have helped many of us learn how to walk, so to speak; but now because they are so deeply rooted and part of us, we would never imagine or think to let them go, so we hobble along, enduring the pain, wagging our spiritual tails and giving kisses. No one knows we're injured. We are broken beyond repair, but we will never choose amputation of a limb on our own. These things and patterns are a part of us! We love them, and we have learned to live with the pain they inflict. Besides, cutting hurts. Pruning hurts!

But there is someone who knows better than us. He wants what's best for us and will cut off what we would never choose to surrender to Him ourselves. The Master knows we will learn to live and walk again. Yes, it will hurt like hell. We will fall, but we will rise again. And once we stumble around in the dark for a minute, we will then begin to see, like Crumpet, we can actually do better with just the remaining three limbs. A lesson in letting go from a little dog named Crumpet; who would have thought!

THE GOD OF QUESTIONS

Jesus is the answer, yet over and over again, throughout the scriptures, we see Him continuously asking questions, 307 of them, to be exact. Now why is that? We know for certain He already knows every thought long before it's ever spoken. On more than one occasion, Jesus responded directly to a thought running through a self-righteous mind and rebuked the thinker who never even uttered a word. He knows; He's always known, so how can absolute knowledge learn anything? Yet He does.

Journey with me if you will, deep beneath the surface layer of our own understanding. Every encounter, every question, and every word spoken by Jesus was not only intentional but predestined. Every question held a purpose, a uniquely cultivated circumstance designed prematurely to elevate our awareness of His identity. God knows, yet he asks. Our High Priest knows everything about us, He knows our going in, our coming out, when we sleep, and when we rise, every hair on our head both numbered and accounted for, yet still He chooses to learn about us. He is, and always will be, the Author of relationships.

From the beginning in the garden to the eternal glory prepared for the Saints, His divine purpose remains immutable. The miraculous was never intended to captivate our attention or incline us toward seeking His hand. The power was, and always is an active display of affection, birthed out of love, flowing in and through relationships. Signs and wonders are not meant to be chased but will follow those that believe, and those who are in a relationship with Him. Intimacy is the elevated awareness, the intended purpose, and the reasoning behind every question. Knowing Him is not just part of the plan, it is the only plan. Intimacy with the Creator is the foundation of creation itself. Far too long, have we been masquerading behind our doctrines and theologies, labeled, staged, and qualified by our impressive knowledge of the scriptures, yet those same scriptures tell us we will be known and marked by our Love, a love for God that overflows into a genuine love for others. This is what sets us apart. This is what makes us sons and daughters of God. This is the great commission and call of God over ALL believers.

We don't need to have all the answers, we need to model after Christ and start asking some questions. Learning, even if we already know, and taking the time to be intentional. Provision isn't in His hand, it's at his feet. The miraculous doesn't come by chasing after an achieved status of faith, but by seeking His face. Everything you will ever need or desire will be gifted and birthed through and out of relationships. Presence is the highest position of power, and intimacy through relationships, illustrates the purpose of our existence.

James 1:19-20: "My dear brothers and sisters, take note of this: Everyone should be quick to listen, slow to speak, and slow to become angry because human anger does not produce the righteousness that God desires."

Challenge: What would change if we began listening to others to learn from them? How has the Lord continued to learn about me?

Prayer: God, help me to listen to learn. May I not enter into conversations with an agenda, especially a religious one, but instead, may I listen to love and understand. Teach me how to ask the right questions. In Jesus' name, Amen.

LOVING MYSELF

Why do I, or should I love myself? Growing up in a religious environment, I confused loving myself with pride. I assumed self-love was arrogance and learned very early on to steer clear of promoting myself in any way. I was terrified of judgmental fingers being pointed in my direction, so instead, I chose to shrink back from the spotlight of God's identity, living in the shadows of others, and occasionally being recognized by family members. This was no better than dumpster diving for leftover approval and although momentarily it brought acceptance, it soon faded, and I found myself in another trash can.

I wonder how many of us shopped at the same store and bought the same lie somewhere along the way? I chose to reject myself first before anyone else could. Instead of finding my identity in God, I searched for my self-worth in people. I stood taller with their praise but crumbled under their criticism, continuing a cycle of broken relationships, always needing, but never receiving enough to be satisfied. I settled for poppers instead of princes because I didn't understand my Royal blood inheritance. I was bound by the lies of religion yet longed for the freedom of grace. My desperation was driving me crazy, and while setting higher standards seemed the right thing to do, it was hard to raise a bar to which I didn't believe I measured up.

But God was calling my name. He was calling me higher than my unmet expectations and sloppy seconds. He began to raise the bar, not on a standard to meet me, but on the standard of me. He began speaking both into and over my life declaring the righteousness I had in Christ Jesus. I didn't have to dress up my darkness or spray perfume on my rotting casket to masquerade around the corpse of a false façade; I was enough, skeletons and all because He is! He died so that I didn't have to stand in shame cowering under the world's standards any longer, but instead, I could stand tall and fully confident on both the Rock of Ages and the rock that was rolled to resurrect my identity. I love myself because he demonstrated real love.

He laid his life down so that I could begin to live mine; He not only raised every standard but met them all as they raised His body on that tree. When he defeated death, Hell, and the grave, and was resurrected, He brought that same resurrecting power to me. He stamped His forever approval and acceptance over my life, and in doing so, also stamped out every opinion and rejection of this world. I will never be any more loved, chosen, forgiven, or called than I am right now in this moment, and I can honestly say I love me because he loves me, and I am everything because He said so! So now I can give without regret, love without limits, and be all that He called me to be, not settling for mediocrity, but rocking the crown of royalty! I refuse to accept anything less than the best He has already predestined for me.

Peter 2:9: "But you are not like that, for you are a chosen people. You are royal priests, a holy nation, God's very own possession. As a result, you can show others the goodness of God, for he called you out of the darkness into his wonderful light."

Challenge: Do I find it hard to love myself? What lies has the enemy used as bait in destroying my identity?

Prayer: God, I have no hope in loving others if I fail to love myself. Expose the lies of the enemy. Teach me by the power of the Holy Spirit, how to accurately see myself. Restore my blood-bought identity. Remove the trees inhibiting my vision. In Jesus' name, Amen.

FAITH TO FOLLOW

Matthew 28:16-20 NIV
"Then the eleven disciples went to Galilee, to the mountain where Jesus had told them to go. When they saw him, they worshipped him; but some doubted. Then Jesus came to them and said, 'All authority in heaven and on earth has been given to me. Therefore, go and make disciples of all nations, baptizing them in the name of the Father and of the Son and the Holy Spirit, and teaching them to obey everything I have commanded you. And surely I am with you always, to the very end of the age.'"

I love how relevant Scripture is to our daily lives. In the above passage, we see Jesus' hand-picked squad eagerly awaiting their marching orders in Galilee. These eleven men had been with Jesus. They knew Him. Nothing about their relationship with Him was casual. These men had witnessed miracles we will never have the opportunity to read about. They were part of the word that never made the page. This was the inner circle. They shared secrets, meals, and heartaches. They were the chosen ones, the beautifully broken boys that Christ re-named "the fishers of all men." If anyone had the faith to follow, it would have been them. These aren't the front-row seat brothers to the greatest story ever told, or VIP pass members posing for autographs and pictures with Jesus. These men were center stage. They were the co-stars of the main production, and yet, despite their position, they doubted it. They went, they worshipped, and they doubted. All in the same paragraph. They obeyed, they praised, but they still felt fear.

I love the response of Jesus in the face of their fear! He came to them. He didn't rebuke their lack of faith or question their commitment to the mission; look at his response. He lifted the weight of fear and responsibility off of their shoulders and placed it on his own. He reminded and affirmed them once again of whom He was by saying, "All authority in heaven and on earth has been given to me." The responsibility wasn't theirs to carry, it never was, it was his! The faith to follow isn't generated from our gifts, talents, or abilities, it is formulated and fortified through obedience and understanding of who Christ is! He holds the authority, the title, and the greatest position. Their fear gave birth to a faith to follow once responsibility and confidence were placed on the One who called them into the great commission.

We have the same mandate on our lives as the original squad, but how many of us are stuck in the same cycle as the disciples? We go, we worship, and we doubt. We say, "Here I am Lord, use me," we get pumped up during worship, and then we hesitate. Did God really speak? We pack our bags for purpose, and then fear knocks on the door with an excuse, resurrecting doubts and questioning our abilities, all the while reminding us of our disqualifying attributes. This is why our faith to follow cannot be mustered up by ourselves. Feelings, even when they are on fire, will eventually burn themselves out. When we chase our own purpose instead of His purpose, we can lose sight of the great commission altogether, which is to know Him, and to make Him known! Not in effort, but in effortlessly being willing, while God dictates the outcome. Faith to follow is inviting Jesus into the fear. It's trusting and learning who He is in every situation and circumstance, and then attaching that revelation to our feet.

Romans 10:15: And how will anyone go and tell them without being sent? That is why the Scriptures say, "How beautiful are the feet of Messengers who bring the good news!"'

Challenge: Where do you feel God is leading you? What steps, if any, have you taken in response?

Prayer: God, take me out of my comfort zone; I'm willing to obey. Give me dreams and visions for my future and the faith to follow. In Jesus' name, Amen.

PEACE, BE STILL!

The storms that come rolling into our lives can be as unpredictable as the weather. Some we see coming just over the horizon, and others we watch from a distance for weeks on end, anticipating their arrival and preparing for their entrance into our lives. Then there are still the select few, the unexpected monsters of mass destruction that always seem to pop up out of nowhere, capable of not only invoking panic and fear but also packing the power to shake our faith and can cause us to lose our footing.

Storms are impossible to escape! They are coming, whether we want them to or not, and unless you are a modern-day version of Elijah, you may not be able to pray away the rain, but you can begin to prepare. I've seen heaven's intervention throughout the world in many different forms, but the most consistent gift I've witnessed being handed out is peace. God will either speak peace to your storm, or speak peace to you in the storm, but either way, the gift is always available. The hardest thing I had to come to grips with as a believer is that we don't always get the storm rebuked. Some of God's best work is done in the dark; it's where we learn to trust; it's where our faith is built into something more than just a cute coffee cup quote or ideology. We don't always get to choose the path less painful, but we always have access to peace within the winds and waves. So often have I seen believers so fixated after witnessing Jesus speaking peace be still to someone else's storm, that they completely missed the peace that is available to them in their storm.

When we are consumed with comparison and expectation, we can miss out on the miracle available to us in the middle. It's the same peace! It's the same gift, they're just wrapped differently! One thing about storms is that when you're in them, it's hard to see clearly. Pain and fear have a funny way of clouding our judgment and blurring our vision. Sometimes, we have to just step back, breathe, and ask God to fix our focus. When we focus on the Storm, that's all we begin to see, but when we focus on Jesus, we're then able to experience the gift of peace within the storm. He will move some mountains, while others we will be forced to climb. Either way, the mountain still switches positions in the end.

Peace is the unopened gift of many, and the oftentimes forfeited miracle of the middle. "Peace, be still!" are the words whispering within the rain, and the gift riding in as the thunder roars. Can you hear it? Just remember the last words Jesus spoke to the disciples before they encountered the storm: "We are going to the other side." God bless!

John 14:27: "I am leaving you with a gift—peace of mind and heart. And the peace I give is a gift the world cannot give. So don't be troubled or afraid."

2 Thessalonians 3:16: "Now may the Lord of Peace himself give you his peace at all times and in every situation. The Lord be with you all."

John 3:16: "For this is how God loved the world: He gave his one and only Son so that everyone who believes in him will not perish but have eternal life."

Challenge: How do I, typically, respond in a crisis? Do I panic anxiously, or do I trust and rest? How would my life be different during difficult seasons if I grasped the gift of peace made available through Christ?

Prayer: Jesus, I'm guilty of not always trusting You with my storms and have often forfeited my gift of peace. Help me to trust You in every situation, especially the hard ones. I need your gift of peace. In Jesus' name, Amen.

REAL LOVE HAS LIMITS

I heard an illustration, yesterday, that blew my mind because it painted the perfect picture of heaven's enforced boundaries. Steven Furtick said, "When you have a dog that you love, and you want him to enjoy freedom without killing himself, or accidentally becoming someone else's pet by running away, you build him a fence." The fence isn't placed out of cruelty or need for control, but rather out of love, care, and a serious concern for the dog's well-being.

I think that a common misconception we have as believers about God's love is when we take the truth of its limitless capacity and equate that as meaning *no limits whatsoever!* Although God's love is limitless, and we will never be more loved than we are right now at this very moment, inside of limitless affection also lies order, structure, and discipline. I think, far too often we behave like spiritually spoiled children who, when God places us inside a protected and secured fenced area that we don't particularly like or understand, out of our misguided perceptions we pout and complain instead of seeing it as a blessing and protection. We then view His limitations and love as a prison sentence. Until we understand that a good father would never knowingly consent or cosign for anything that could potentially cause harm or lead to his children's death, we will continue to view his grace and mercy as judgment and control, and we will feel punished instead of parented!

Love without limits is not only dangerous and destructive but is selfish and codependent at its core. Boundaries, however, are proof of our value. You only guard and put a fence around something important to you. That can be either yourself or someone else. Rest assured that real love has limits, and it's a hedge of protection, not a prison sentence!

Job 1:10: "You have always put a wall of protection around him and his home and his property. You have made him prosper in everything he does. Look how rich he is!"

Challenge: How do you view God's boundaries (fence)? Do you view them as protection or a prison sentence? Why?

Prayer: Lord, thank you for the hedge of protection you have placed in my life. Help me to see your loving boundaries as protection, instead of a prison. I'm so sorry for being rebellious and for running outside of your loving limits. Teach me how to flourish inside of the parameters of purpose you have given me. You are a good father and I'm so thankful for your fence of protection. Amen.

LESS OF ME, AND MORE OF YOU

Less of me, and more of you...
But lately, that's been really hard to do...
Visions blurred, broken glass
Reflections of a shattered past...
Moving forward, still chained to pain
Yesterday's demons still calling my name
Trying to run, chasing after your freedom
Tripping over soul ties, why can't I just leave 'em?
You said I have purpose, and that you have plans for me...
Is this really the woman you planned that I'd be?
You tell me you love me; you say I'm forgiven...
But that don't make any sense... God, you see how I'm livin'
Addicted to approval; I'll do damn near anything to get it
Strung out on attention like a crackhead chasing the next hit
I'd rather have my fix than allow you to you fix me
I don't understand... God, why won't you just miss me...
Pass me up... God, I know you'll find better
Somebody else, not wearing this scarlet-stained sweater
I've burned the bridge, God you know this won't last!
Don't you remember all the times I've left in the past?
Empty promises, broken connection; I always leave you for another man's affection.
I can't comprehend why you even still try.
Every time I say I love you; you know it's a lie!
Why won't you just deuce me, cut me off, and be through...
You already know ahead of time what I'm about to do!
I'll give you a little, then I'll snatch it right back; I'm always the dope fiend running back to the sac...
I know your ways better, your words give me life
But I'm still standing here bleeding, holding the knife
Fighting the enemy, the inner me and I'm losing

Alarms going off, but I still choose to keep snoozing
The struggle is real, God, and I'm knee-deep in it
The battle is yours, but I'm still determined to win it...
My way's the highway, GPS destination set on Hell
Pain became my pen and now that's the only story I'll tell...
I keep writing myself out, but you keep writing me back in...
You white out my past, your blood keeps covering my sins
Thirsty and hungry, I'm out here eatin' on anything but you
Leftover love is about the best I can do...
You want a commitment, but I'm good with no strings attached...
This junky monkey is getting heavy, and it's breaking my back!
I want to let go, but my mind's my prison,
Mindsets and strongholds have stolen my vision
Blind and broken, I'm now just a beggar...
But you came with keys and you stripped off that sweater
You took my hand and showed me to my seat...
You brought me to the table, and taught me to eat,
You prepared a feast for me in front of my haters
Now goodness and mercy became my only waiters
This prodigal daughter finally made her way back
Beauty for ashes... there's no going back!

BROKEN CISTERNS

I once heard that when you are very thirsty, you tend to look for substitutes. How true that is! When I'm lonely, I have settled for less than love. When I'm fearful, I have taken the back door quietly. When I'm ashamed, I tend to hide rather than risk exposure. And when I'm overly confident, I start living for the praises of men rather than for the approval of the One.

We all have these substitutes, places we go (a relationship God gifts us) to draw water that won't sustain us. In reverse, we can even take a good thing (relationship) and attempt to intertwine it with our own broken system. This can oftentimes leave us drained and them empty.

Until we go to the Source, the Well that never will run dry, we will continue to search, seeking for substitutes to quench a thirst that we can never fill. We can take a "God thing" and destroy it because we make the thing into a god. We come to the relationship half-empty, seeking our wholeness from the gift rather than the Giver of the gift.

When we allow ourselves to go to the True Source for filling, we unconsciously and unknowingly raise the standard. Substitutes no longer suit the palate, and we become quicker to spit them out. As we seek and chase the living water which flows from the endless spring of God's eternal love, we will never again be thirsty!

John 4:13-14: "Everyone who drinks of this water will thirst again, but whoever drinks of the water that I shall give him shall never thirst, but the water that I shall give him shall become in him a well of water springing up to eternal life."

Challenge: What broken cisterns have you substituted for truth? Is it porn in a not-so-good marriage? An extra donut to feed a feeling? Auctioning your self-worth to the highest bidder or trying to reinvent yourself in someone else's shadow? What has been the result of running to substitutes when you are thirsty?

Prayer: God, I know You, and You alone are capable of meeting my needs, wants, and desires. I haven't always turned to You in my desperate attempts to satisfy my soul, and that has left me thirsty and empty. I know you offer living water. Teach me how to bring all my needs into your presence. In Jesus' name, Amen.

UNREALISTIC EXPECTATIONS

None of us are strangers to heartbreaks and soul scars. We all have long lists of disappointments, fears, and frustrations. The what-ifs, if only and regrets become the baggage dragged into future relationships, business opportunities, and ministry. These are the battle scars that tell our stories. The wounds of experience that have tainted our hands and hearts for good. There's no antidote or cute quote as remedies for these memories. These are the life lessons that burned our hearts and branded our souls indefinitely! We are broken vessels. All of us! We are wounded warriors at our best, and if left untreated will bleed over people who didn't cut us. Hurt people hurt people and that's the truth.

So how do we recover? How do we heal in a way that our old heart scars don't inflict new wounds on others? How do we bounce back after being broken to our core? I've been on this crazy healing journey for a while now and it sucks! Picking up the pieces of our pain is never fun. Putting Humpty Dumpty back together again is a job that only the King can do. He doesn't just superglue our wounds. We don't get a quick fix and then get to be used. Piece by piece we examine the entire process together and reflect on, "How did I get here? What led up to this heartache and what am I going to do about it now?"

As I've traced the maze of pain back to its root, I've found that a lot of my mismanaged hurt began in a place of unrealistic expectations. I've put them on myself, people, and God. and in doing so have experienced heartbreak I was never intended to have. I have been bitter, busted, and betrayed all behind an expectation that wasn't mine to assign. I have put my faith, hope, and confidence fully in an outcome instead of trusting the

Author of my existence in the process. This is where I've fallen. These are the bruised knees I could have avoided if I'd trusted more and expected less. Boiled down, its faith misplaced. I've put my faith in people, positions, outcomes, and feelings and all of these are recipes for a heart attack.

So how do we break the cycle of insanity? How do we love and serve minus the sickness of expectation? We have to trust! We cannot stop trusting just because we have been burned and bruised! If expectation dies, hope dies, and our light grows weary and dim. So how is it then that expectation is the answer and the problem all at the same time?! My faith, hope, and expectations all need a divorce from the experience. My faith and expectation must become married to the King of my circumstance. I need to fully understand and make peace with my pain. The King of the Palace is also the King of the pit, and that's the hole which none of us ever expected to be. Our trust cannot be tied to our current circumstances or feelings. We will miss it, or we will quit in the process! We will let go of people that God has positioned in our lives because we will attach an expectation to their behavior, instead of trusting God with them fully! We will self-sabotage our blessings because our faith is attached to feelings, and we will follow our heart's desires straight to hell.

Follow your heart, that's what the world says, but my Bible says the heart is deceitful and desperately sick. Who can understand it? (Jeremiah 17:9). If we have any hope at getting this thing right, getting relationships right, ministry right, business deals right, and living the life God has called us to flourish in, we have to trust what he is doing! We have to trust that he has better for us than the things we expect for and from ourselves. Myles Munroe has a quote that says, "When the expectation of a thing is unknown, abuse is inevitable." If I could add to that quote or remix it, I would say, "Where expectation is misplaced, abuse is inevitable." We have to learn to trust what God is doing in the process. We have to put our preferences, feelings, desires, and expectations on the altar of absolute trust. We need His permission to pursue all that we do. We must trust in the process, not in the outcome, knowing that no matter what happens, He is working it out for our good and his glory, regardless! His plans for us always far exceed the plans and purposes we design and imagine for ourselves.

Now faith is confidence in what we hope for and assurance about what we do not see. **Hebrews 11:1:** our only hope is to have our expectations fully placed and planted in Christ. This is the only expectation that gives life and gives it to the fullest! Trust Him! Trust Him with the pain! It's all part of the plan we cannot yet see. Our wounds and scars will then become the platform for every life we encounter and will become the medicine used to bring healing to the world!

Challenge Question: How have I experienced heartache from having unrealistic expectations? Is my faith only married to the outcome or am I faithful no matter what the outcome?

Prayer: God, teach me how to divorce myself from unrealistic expectations. Show me what it looks like to be faithful even when my expectations have not been fulfilled. Help me to learn that You are enough and to be satisfied with where I am. Here, the present, in this very moment, is holy. Help me live, breathe, and move in this space right in front of me. Expecting nothing but Your presence, the greatest gift of all. Amen.

TRADING PERFECTION FOR EXCELLENCE!

Perfection not only sets impossible standards, but she also strives to impart those same standards to others. Perfection, herself, is never satisfied and those who embark with her on that journey, often find themselves depleted and deprived. She will waste your time, energy, and resources, and when you're empty, or should I say thirsty, almost anything will begin to satisfy you. When nothing's ever good enough, or measures up to perfection's standards, any person with a pulse and a compliment can quench a need we may not even be aware that we have.

Excellence, on the other hand, wears her robe of royalty with confidence! Instead of setting an unattainable standard, she becomes the standard. She is the definition of true virtue and beauty. Excellence gives her best, but her expectations are kept to herself. Excellence will always call you higher but offers her own hands to pull you up! She is nothing like Perfection who always seeks approval, and control and needs to be pleased. She is complete, whole, and self-reliant, and many find themselves pleased just to be in her royal presence. Excellence isn't a standard to be met, but a mindset of grace that has already been attained!

When our eyes are fixed on Jesus Christ, the truest example of perfection, we can stop striving to be, and just become. We can forgo the meaningless pursuit of attempting to attain perfection, and rest in the excellent finished work of the cross! The standard of perfection has already been reached so that we don't have to strive to attain righteousness, but can instead work from a place of Grace, ever so elegantly becoming excellent! What a gift! I'll take excellence over perfection any day!

2 Corinthians 8:7: "But as you excel in everything—in faith, in speech, in knowledge, in all earnestness, and in our love for you—see that you excel in this act of grace also."

Challenge: Have I been operating in any areas of my life with a spirit of perfectionism? How has the spirit of perfectionism affected my relationships (self/others)? How would my life be different if I traded perfection for excellence?

Prayer: Abba, You are the only perfection this world knows. I fall short, even on my best days. Teach me how to operate from a spirit of excellence, giving my best, while extending grace to others. Help me work from a place of victory, knowing I will never be perfect, but I will strive to excel with the gifts you have given me. In Jesus' name, Amen.

DELAYED DOESN'T MEAN DENIED

Jesus and Lazarus were tight. They were good friends and did fellowship together often as Jesus was a frequent house guest. In John's Gospel, he describes the plea of Mary and Martha (Lazarus's sisters) as "the one you love is very sick." This lets us know for absolute certain, there was nothing casually committed about this relationship.

Jesus loved Lazarus; this was his dear friend, yet when He receives the news of his illness and impending death, at this point, everyone else's knowledge solely depended on his presence and willingness to intervene, the healer, the answer and the cure himself stayed where he was for two more days. Why would he do that? Why would He let his friend, whom He dearly loved suffer any longer than he had to? Why didn't He come immediately? What kind of love turns its back on those it cares about? We love to say in church that God is always on time. Well, whose time is He on? He definitely wasn't on Mary and Martha's time, and I'm pretty sure if we could have asked Lazarus, he wouldn't have considered Him just fashionably late. Jesus was MIA in the middle of a crisis, and then what was already bad, got worse; Lazarus died.

Jesus had sent word back to Mary and Martha upon their desperate cries for his intervention, a promise to them that their brother's sickness would not end in death but that the glory of the Lord may be revealed. But then Lazarus died, despite the word from the Word, and despite the promise, Lazarus was gone. Their anticipation, faith-filled declaration of healing, spoken and promised to them by the Healer himself was now no more than an unmet expectation.

They believed, and trusted fully, that Jesus would come through for them like He always had before, but not this time! This time, they faced the dual hardship of rejection and heartache.

The reality began to set in that maybe this Jesus was not who they thought He was, and they were right. Despite their limited understanding and human perspective, this was His intended purpose from the very beginning. He is never what we think, He is always greater, always higher, and always challenging our inaccurate belief systems and errant theologies. His mission was not to meet their limited expectation of who He was but to challenge their capacity for His true identity. What kind of love turns His back on those He claims to care about? Not healing love! Healing love is comfortable, healing love feels good, healing love is on time and leaves its immediate mark.

But there is another type of love, a higher love, an uncomfortable and unbearable delayed, far beyond our understanding type of love, that also leaves its mark. Jesus bears the mark of this delayed type of Love that also turned its back in the moment of His greatest suffering. Jesus also resisted this type of love while in the flesh of His humanity as He pleaded with His Heavenly Father to remove the cup of suffering. This is resurrection love. Resurrection love bypasses feelings, drives over disappointments, and shatters our expectations. This love is not preferable but purposeful. It's not a band-aid or a watered-down version of what we think love is in the moment of our greatest pain. Resurrection love hurts both the giver and the receiver temporarily for the greater good and Glory of God to be manifested in and through our lives.

Lazarus did die when Jesus promised he would live. Both are true. God's greatest work in our lives begins in the tomb of our disappointments, dead dreams, doubts, and unmet expectations. It is the dank and disappointing dark room of development where everything in us must die first to truly live. Many of us identify with or find ourselves in this same type of predicament that Mary and Martha faced. We have been believing in God for breakthroughs, miracles, provision, and healing but instead, we feel ghosted, denied, and disappointed in the middle of a process we can't comprehend or understand. I want to encourage you, with Lazarus as my witness, that delayed does not necessarily mean denied.

As you gaze upon the valley of your dry bones, disappointments, dead dreams, and dusty expectations, hear the Word of the Lord to you today: come forth! He is breathing into every dead and dried-up space and calling you to live. Your temporary delay and disappointment are for reappointment! This sickness will not end in death but so that the glory of the Lord may be revealed. Jesus spoke this word over Lazarus and then he died. I believe he is speaking the same thing over every one of us today. We are being developed and learning self-discipline in this season AKA the tomb of dead expectations, disappointment, and doubt to bring us into a greater and higher understanding of who He is. Resurrection Love is here!

John 11:40-44: "Then Jesus said, 'Did I not tell you that if you believe, you will see the glory of God?'" So, they took away the stone. Then Jesus looked up and said, "Father, I thank you that you have heard me. I knew that you always hear me, but I said this for the benefit of the people standing here, that they may believe that you sent me." When he had said this, Jesus called in a loud voice, "Lazarus, come out!" The dead man came out, his hands and feet wrapped with strips of linen, and a cloth around his face. Jesus said to them, "Take off the grave clothes and let him go."'

Challenge: What's inside your tomb? What dreams, relationships, and ideas have you, in a sense, laid to rest? Do you believe that God can resurrect everything inside your tomb? Do you even believe that he desires you to experience resurrection? Why or why not?

Prayer: Daddy God, there are dreams, ideas, and relationships that have all died. They are locked away and buried. If I'm honest, a part of me doubts your ability and willingness to resurrect them. Sometimes it's easier for me to just move on than to face the funeral head-on. Lord, help me learn from the example of Lazarus that you are still rolling stones. Speak to my dead spaces and call forth life. I believe in the resurrection power available to me through Jesus Christ! Do what only You can do! In Jesus' name, Amen.

IN HIS PRESENCE

I've searched the world over but never did find
A love so sweet, intentional, and divine
I ran high and low in arms and streets
Overwhelmed and exhausted while beating my feet
I gave my all, time and time again
When compromise was needed, I would always bend
Motivations were high but with standards too low
I would pour out my all and still have nothing to show
I lived to love and loved to live
But a counterfeit version is all I could give
Insecurities and strongholds kept me in sin
Envisioning the victory but never managing a win
I knew all the answers... Her name was Pride
She held the key to my closet where my skeletons reside
Locked down and hidden, with no chance of escape
Life sucked from my soul, disappearing as vape
Longing for freedom, I ran after wells
Chasing the dragon, deceived by her spells
Desperately thirsty... yet nothing would quench
Ashamed and broken, I sat on Well's bench
In the heat of the day, so that no one would see
While searching for water, Living Water found me
He asked a simple question, my response, well thought out
As my tongue spit out answers, justifying my drought
He bypassed my excuses and lifted my head
He knew the names of every man I'd ever had in my bed
He asked for a drink, His presence revealed
As He pulled back the covers on all I'd concealed
Concerned without judgment, He told me the truth
He traced back my emptiness down to its root
He showed me the empty spaces I'd been so desperate to fill
Could only be accomplished inside His will
While dried up and thirsty lost and deceived

The Answer to my depravity chose to find me
He gave me a purpose and called me by name
One drink from His fountain has changed the whole game
No longer desperately searching to find
A love so sweet, intrinsically defined
While at Hell's well, Jesus found me
Already sitting in the dirt left me positioned at his feet
So now I keep running back to those wells
No longer for a drink, but with a story to tell
Jesus met me in the middle of my mess and brought me through
And if He came for me... He'll come for you too!

GOLIATHS FALL

Submit yourselves, then, to God. Resist the devil, and he will flee from you **(James 4:7 NIV).**

In my limited experience with ministries, especially those that primarily focus on deliverance, I've heard a lot of talk about resistance. The more you feed your spirit, the less your flesh gets to acting up. We love to go to war with the enemy, snatching back territory and seeing our Goliaths fall. We are quick to grab our oil, plead the blood of Jesus over our issues and bind and break both curses and strongholds. We love to get loud, suited, and booted and stand chest out with our swords. We quote scriptures like bullets and prophesy the victory we have in Jesus, decreeing and declaring our wins. Yet, despite all of our efforts, we only manage to knock Goliath down for a season, only for him to show back up, dressed differently, but coming at us, nonetheless.

As I've reflected over my own struggles, strongholds, and sin patterns, taking a closer look at James 4:7, I realized I'd spent much more time and energy resisting than I actually did submitting. Temporary relief and seasons of abstinence are not true freedom. No matter how many times we knock Goliath down, he will continue to get up, unless we do like David and cut off his head. As I prayed through this and asked God what it looks like to take the head off Goliath for good, the Holy Spirit led me to the first part of James 4:7. "Submit yourselves, then, to God."

We have no hope of resisting until we have first submitted. We can go to war all we want, and we can say all the right things, but we will never get the head of the enemy until Jesus has the hearts of His warriors. Freedom and victory are found on our faces, and at His feet.

Challenge: What is the Goliath (sin) in your life that you can't seem to kill, no matter how hard you try? Are you resisting without submission? What do I feel like the Holy Spirit is asking from me, and am I willing to surrender?

Abba: Father, God, there are sin patterns in my life that keep creeping in. Resistance seems to work for a season. Show me by the power of the Holy Spirit, what a submitted heart looks like. Teach me how to fight on my face and at your feet. Help me put to death all the patterns and mindsets standing between me and your purpose. In Jesus' name, Amen.

CHANGE GONNA COME

One thing that is always guaranteed to come is change. Not many like it. You don't always see it coming, but change is inevitable. What exactly is our beef with change anyway? Why all the anxiety and poked ant-pile mindset over something that is outside our realm of control the majority of the time? Why do we almost worship and run to the places and things we've found and labeled as comfortable? What is it about the path of least resistance that we find so attractive?

Growth only comes from change, and even though we know this, we resent and push back the process purposefully and intentionally. We resist change like it's an actual growth of cancer and run from the one thing that promises to propel us toward our purpose.

The unknown is a scary place, and unfortunately, that's where the root of change resides. Fortunately, though, for us, faith is fear's next-door neighbor. In this mixed environment, the potential is birthed. Somewhere between fear and faith lies the choice to embrace change and trust the Maker's Master Plan.

This is the place where we relinquish control to gain control of our lives. We take one blind step of total surrender, only to be met with ten steps of lasting security. We trade our limited knowledge for God's unlimited Higher Knowledge that He knows, and that's enough. CHANGE GONNA COME. I hope, not only for your sake but mine, that it comes soon because we will both get a blessing on the backside of our becoming.

CHANGE: the one thing I both love and hate... yet always appreciate, eventually.

"JESUS CHRIST IS THE SAME YESTERDAY AND TODAY, YES, AND FOREVER" (**Hebrews 13:8**).

Challenge Question: How do I feel about change? Has my attitude towards change ever prolonged the actual process?

Prayer: Dear Jesus, I know change is inevitable. I know growth is only possible through change. Help me to embrace the process of becoming. In Jesus' name, Amen.

CONSUMING 🔥 FIRE 🔥

Therefore, since we are receiving a kingdom that cannot be shaken, let us be thankful, and so worship God acceptably with reverence and awe, for our "God is a consuming fire" Hebrews 12: 28-29.

So, be aware today that it is the Lord your God who is crossing over ahead of you as a consuming fire. He will destroy them, and He will subdue them before you, so that you may drive them out and eliminate them quickly, just as the Lord has spoken to you Deuteronomy 9:3.

Have you ever stopped to wonder why some things and some relationships just don't work, no matter what you try to do? You could be all in, giving 110% percent and fully committed, and yet somehow, someway, it still manages to fall apart! As I've been meditating over these two verses, the Holy Spirit gave me a revelation that really hit hard and home. God's children (believers) have the inheritance of heavenly protection so that when God goes before us as an all-consuming fire, He eliminates and burns out everything and everyone that He hasn't already marked for us! If it isn't from Him, it's destined to fail. Fire burns out imperfections and removes the things that can be shaken until all that is left is pure gold (the unshakable).

We can try our ways all we want, and we can get into things and relationships that aren't for us and beg God to bless them until we are blue in the face, but in the end, we will only end up out of breath and completely exhausted. His fire is all-consuming! You can stand in front of the things and people you are so desperate to keep, with a fire extinguisher, but when standing in front of the all-consuming fire of God coming straight at your soul, best believe your best attempts to hold Him back will only temporarily delay the inevitable! He not only goes before us, but He also works within us, striking a match and burning to the ground everything that is not of Him.

I've tried fighting off the fire for years, but instead of being consumed, I ended up burned and scarred! My hands and my heart are both charred from my resistance, and the pain of resistance is far worse than the pain of purification. I'm done being burned! I'm done with self-inflicted wounds due to my disobedience! I want to burn and be so consumed by the love of God that I can look at what I think I need and desire, and say, "If it's not of You, or from You, I don't even want it anymore! Burn it out!" I'm done sitting in a pile of ashes crying over the remains of decisions I've made without Him, and I'm ready to be completely consumed in His Holy Blaze! Fire also catches things on fire, and that's the kind of life we have been called to live as believers!

Challenge: What vices/relationships have you been holding onto, knowing that God wants to remove them? Why are you having a hard time letting them go?

Prayer: God, I know there are things and people I refuse to let go of. Holding on hurts, but I'm scared of what my life will look like without them. God, I'd rather be scared than scarred, so today with Your help, I am willing to let them go. Jesus, please fill the void in my heart that their absence will leave. Fill me, mold me, renew me. In Jesus' name, Amen.

FAMILIARITY BREEDS COMPLACENCY

When amazement and wonder get replaced by familiarity and casual commitment, miracles are often missed, by way of complacency. In Mark, chapter 6, Jesus gathers his crew and takes a road trip to his hometown of Nazareth. Now at first, the people are amazed, as they can clearly see that this guy's got something special. He's gifted! He's different! He must be important! But when someone leaks the truth about this guy's past, the leaders of the church board start talking amongst themselves and come to a unanimous conclusion. He's just Jesus, a carpenter, and a nobody. Instant rejection! Now get this - their offense, rejection, disapproval, and indifference, blinded them to the fact that He was anointed by God, and due to their unbelief and familiarity in which they viewed Jesus, this limited the power of God from working in and through their lives. They missed their miracles, their words, their blessings, and their breakthroughs, all because they tripped over something in His past. They disqualified someone God had already given His stamp of approval.

Their rejection of Him, ultimately only hurt them. Jesus, himself was amazed at their unbelief, and in verse 4 he said to them, "A prophet is not without honor and respect except in his hometown and among his relatives and his household." It goes on in verse 5 to say that he could not perform a miracle at all because of their unbelief, except that He laid His hands on a few people and healed them. Are we getting this? This is God! Their rejection of Jesus who is sent by God tied his hands. He couldn't give them what they needed, because they couldn't get over who He was. His own family had a problem with Him! They couldn't spot and call out the anointing of God over his life.

Sometimes, it's the people who are closest to us whose approval matters the most, and who reject what God is doing in our lives. They can't see it! They stumble across a memory and dismiss the gift, and in doing so, their judgment of you prevents the power of God from working through you in their lives. What a bummer! Listen, do not let someone's rejection of you stop you. They're not in a position to strip you of any titles, talents, and gifts that they did not give you themselves! Jesus intentionally took this road trip with his crew to show them what happens when people reject the gift and calling of God over their lives. Jesus took them to Nazareth, knowing in advance He would be rejected, and used the rejection as ministry training. This is the place they were commissioned and anointed for service.

Jesus took the place of some of his greatest pain and turned it into a platform for discipleship training. He then goes on to say, and I'm paraphrasing, if people reject you, they reject me and ultimately, they reject themselves. Shake them off (remix for the 20th century). Jesus told his disciples to shake them haters off! Verse 11 says, "Any place that does not welcome you, or listen to you when you leave there, shake the dust off the soles of your feet as a testimony against them breaking all ties with them because they rejected my message." It's their loss! Not yours! Shake off their opinions, indifference, rejections, disapproval, and offenses. It's poison! And it becomes a prison! Don't let it get into your system! Don't get stuck and build a house in a place you were only meant to pass through! You have nothing to prove to anyone (pigs don't deserve your pearls or your pity), so move on until the miraculous carried within you is met with amazement, honor, and wonder. Here is where you dig in, plant your feet, and flourish!

Mark 6:4-6: "Jesus said to them, 'A prophet is not without honor except in his own town, among his relatives and in his own home.' 5. He could not do any miracles there, except lay his hands on a few sick people and heal them. 6. He was amazed at their lack of faith."

Challenge: Has anyone ever discredited you based on your past? What was the result?

Prayer: Father, You have blessed me with gifts and anointing for kingdom purposes. Help me to know when I'm wasting my time and prostituting my calling on people who are unable to receive it. Lead me in my exits by the power of your spirit. Give me the strength and wisdom to know when it's time to go. In Jesus' name, Amen.

THE FINAL SAY

Blinded by man's wisdom
Theology blurs our sight
Walking in "Godly" counsel
As doctrines dim our light
Debating over scriptures
While revelations slip away
Concerned more with being right
Than knowing the right thing to say
Shackled to our intelligence
Barred behind our thoughts
Religion would rather prove you wrong
Than minister reconciliation to the lost
When motives seek exposure
Their assignments straight from Hell
They would rather have rocks to throw
Than patiently sit waiting by the well...
Behold the adulterous woman
Religions dragged her through our streets
They have labeled her unworthy
And now they've thrown her at our feet
One by one we can throw stones
Or we can choose to walk away...
We can cover her, in the middle of the dirt
Let's let love have the final say

HE RESTED ON DAY SEVEN

God spoke universes into existence. With breath behind His syllables, the sun is still stuck in the same place that He spoke it into at the moment of its creation, and Man, formed from dust, received that same breath, becoming an Image bearer of His Glory. The Potter spun and created on the wheel of eternity, and Creation's rhythm was set in motion, continuing throughout the end time. He is the master, both inside and separate from all He has created, yet, in all of his infinite power, God decided to blow the referee whistle on round seven and call a time-out. Why? Did the moon maker get too tired and need a break? Did the creation-conductor, the destination-driver, the Beetlejuice-breather, and the earth's Creator grow weary?

When we assume we were created for a system, instead of knowing that the system was actually created for us, we become attached to methods that enslave us, instead of rhythms that revive us. Rest was never meant to be a requirement met religiously, but rather a request met graciously, trusting that the Master set this momentum with intention, not for His relief, but for our regeneration. The system starter shrank Himself down to demonstrate His Divine design by representing Himself inside His own created system. The first repetition of rest in the grand symphony of grace was demonstrated by Him. Rest was His rightful reward for a job well done, and if we refrain from a religious system, we can reap the reward of rest just the same.

Can we cultivate the same awestruck wonder that captivated the heart of God, which invited the Creator to back up and just breathe in a job well done? Rest is not a requirement to fulfill but is required if we were going to walk in the complete fullness of who He created and called us to be, and if He rested on seven, then so should we.

Genesis: 2:1-3: "Thus, the heavens and the earth were completed in all their vast array. By the seventh day God had finished the work he had been doing; so on the seventh day, he rested from all his work. Then God blessed the seventh day and made it holy because on it he rested from all the work of creating that he had done."

Mark 2:27-28: "Then he said to them, 'The Sabbath was made for man, not man for the Sabbath. So the Son of Man is Lord even of the Sabbath.'"

Prayer: Father, I know you created a day of rest for my benefit. The Sabbath is not a religious duty, but a loving gift. Help me find my rhythm of rest. I want to do my best for myself and everyone around me. I'm sorry for not always trusting in your design. Remind me when I'm offbeat and lead me back into your loving symphony of grace. In Jesus' name, Amen.

UNDERSTANDING I AM

I've been restless, trying to figure out where God went and why He changed up on me, all of a sudden. I thought God was the same yesterday, today, and forever, but He's not. Why is He changing?

I remember when I first got locked up, I would pray for God to let me go. I would make all these promises and contracts (that I would always break), begging for Him to give me grace and let me go. I'd promise Him things like, "I'll never do it again," or "If you just do this for me, I'll do that for You." And it worked!

For a while, God was my genie in a lamp, granting my wishes because He was operating at the level of my understanding. He didn't change. I grew. I used to pray that God would bless me with an extra tray of food. Now, He gives me the power not to eat so much.

God is good. He meets us where we are, and He is to us what we need in that season. Then He pulls the rug out - or the plug, so He can take us to the next level of understanding. I can't keep expecting old blessings as proof He is with me at this moment. As long as I'm looking over my shoulder for God to move, I will miss the very thing He is trying to do right in front of me.

I've changed. Milk can't sustain a grown woman, even though it's the same source that feeds me meat. If I wait for milk, I'll miss the meal and be lacking. Goosebumps and spirit shivers don't equal growth. That's not proof of His presence. "Feel goods" and spiritual suckers are for infants.

When I no longer need a feeling to keep me committed, I'm changing. God does not change or lie... He can't and He won't. He will never deny who He is. However, my understanding of Him should change as fast and frequently as I change my underwear. My perception of God and the mystery of this Gospel should unfold a little more each day. I am no longer restless, but relentless in understanding I am.

Hebrews 5: 13-14: "Anyone who lives on milk, being still an infant, is not acquainted with the teaching about righteousness. But solid food is for the mature, who by constant use have trained themselves to distinguish good from evil."

Challenge: List three ways you have matured over this past year. Has your understanding of God changed? (Give an example.)

Prayer: God, I know you are the same yesterday, today, and forever. However, my understanding of you is not. Help me to pursue growth at all costs. Teach me how to feed on the meat of the word. I don't ever want to be satisfied with a milky knowledge of who you are. I want to learn from you every day. I'm asking for revelations, dreams, and visions. In Jesus' name, Amen.

CRUNCH TIME

There are times in all of our walks with God, that I believe He would describe and classify as crunch time. With the pressure on, we have somehow been spiritually shifted into go mode, and the levels of urgency have been redlined! When God is getting ready to take you into something, shift seasons, or open a new door in your life, He frequently will bring us into a season of extreme focus and self-discipline prior to cutting the red ribbon of purpose. He is preparing you to step into something.

Crunches are a very focused exercise. They are repetitive and painful and will also bring maximum results if done correctly. Do you feel as if God has zeroed in on an area in your life and is rapidly prompting obedience time and time again, almost to the point of aggravation and frustration? When God is after an area of our hearts and when we are in crunch mode, the preparation and relentless pressure can almost feel overwhelming at times.

We have to remember when we are in God's gym, and when He has called us out of our exercise routine and into the strenuous spiritual training; it's always in preparation for what's next. Our gut reaction, at least mine, is to tell Him everything I'm already doing in my routine and why it works (like He doesn't know), instead of just offering up my obedience and sacrifice without question. Crunch time sucks, and in the process, I'm usually tired, and sore, and some days, I want to quit! I can't crunch alone. I would never voluntarily put myself in that position, but with God as my guide and with purpose in mind, I can fix my eyes on the prize, forgetting the past, and getting ready for what's ahead.

Crunch time means God's getting you ready because He's about to use you and bring you into something glorious! No pain, no gain, no process, no palace. That's just how our King rolls!

Ephesians 2:10: "For we are God's handiwork, created in Christ Jesus to do good works, which God prepared in advance for us to do."

Ecclesiastes 3:1: "There is a time for everything and a season for every activity under the heavens."

Challenge: What season are you currently in? What is God preparing you for? Make a list of 3 things you should be doing to maximize your growth in this season.

Prayer: Abba, You created seasons in my life for growth. Help me to identify and lean in where you have planted me in this season. May I not run ahead or get left behind. Help me move at the pace of grace. In Jesus' name, Amen.

LOOSE LIPS SINK SHIPS

Proverbs 15:4: *"A soothing tongue speaking words that build up and encourage is a tree of life but a perverse tongue speaking words that overwhelm and depress crushes the spirit."*

When I choose to pick other people apart with my words instead of allowing the Holy Spirit to point to that place in my own heart that's jacked up, I have invited the devil to dinner and paid the bill. I have manipulated my mindset into a judgmental courtroom and appointed myself as their sanctification attorney. And honestly, in their courtroom, I'm out of my jurisdiction. I must resist the urge to tamper with other people's evidence. I am not their court-appointed attorney; the only thing I should be representing, anyhow is Grace. With every finger I point, I must remember there are three pointing back at me. The tongue is a fast talker, and it'll talk me straight to Hell if I let it.

God says that the power of both life and death are each held in that one tiny muscle. He then tells us to choose life. Every muscle in our body has an opposite muscle except for the tongue and the heart, (I wonder why that is). The scripture tells us that out of the abundance of the heart, the mouth speaks. Gossip and greatness cannot coexist in the same room, and one will always drive out the other. Loose lips sink ships, and I can't sail from the bottom of the ocean. Today, I am drawing a line in the sand.

Today, I say, enough is enough, to the ugly that's inside of me. Today, I choose life and everything else must be confronted and ordered to leave! I'm sold out! No more room for messy or petty in this heart's inn!

Challenge: How have I been using my words? Am I edifying others or picking them apart? I challenge you for the next 24 hours to intentionally refrain from speaking negatively or gossiping. Instead, focus on building up everyone around you. See how different your life becomes overnight.

Prayer: Jesus, I surrender my mouth to you. Use me to speak life into others. Teach me how to become a special vessel for your namesake. I repent from gossip and negativity. I want to be marked and known as a woman of character and integrity. Give me the grace to become all you have created me to be. In Jesus' name, Amen.

TAINTED HANDS

My hands are tainted! I've been digging around in the dirt, and it wasn't to plant flowers, dig wells, or search for diamonds! I walked away... out of the palace, down the steps, past the courtyard, away from family, friends, formality, riches, and royal robes, right into pig pens, sloppy seconds, and leftover lunches.

I knew better, but I didn't do better. I hate it here, yet here I am again. I'm caught in a sick cycle of self-isolation from everything that I love. Shame... I really thought she was gone for good, but one stroll down the hood and she's back like a backpack, or maybe a leach. She's driving me crazy and lower all at the same time... She's always on rewind, taking me back to the places I don't want to go. I want to escape! I want to go back. Back to the music, the dancing, and the feasts. I want a seat at the table again. I want a friend. Ohhh-but I'm not worthy!

I abandoned every title, ripped off my robe, and fled unconcerned with the consequences and ripple effects.
I've caused way too much damage and cried wolf, fox, and ferret too many times. That's probably the best description since it's the closest thing I could think of next to a weasel... Conniving, manipulative, and sneaky, I took my inheritance, like the coward I am, just to make friends with monsters in the mud.

BUT WAIT!! What if He takes me back? I could come home and work my way back in. Even Daddy's slaves are being treated with more dignity than this. That's it! I'm going back... But maybe not to my seat at the table. I'm not worthy of that. But maybe... just maybe, he'll give me a dust rag to wipe it clean.

As I nervously approach, He sees me in the distance. BUT WAIT! What is He doing? He's starting to run! I drop to my knees, tears pouring down my face. As He embraces me, He pulls me to my feet and tends to my tears.

"Quick! Get her cleaned and dressed! The finest evening gown and slippers... Hurry up! Someone fetch her robe. And you there, run to town and buy her the finest set of pearls you can find. I believe my daughter mistakenly left the other set with some pigs in the mud."

He kisses my forehead. "Welcome home! I saved your seat at the table. Now go! Get ready. Wash the mud from your hands so we can get this party started. My prodigal daughter was lost, but now she is found! She has come back home!"

My hands are still tainted. I'm still digging in the dirt. I'm planting flowers, digging wells, and searching for lost diamonds. It turns out dirt isn't so bad after all... it just depends on what you do with it.

Verse:
Luke 15 22-24
"But the father said to his servants, 'Quick! Bring the best robe and put it on him. Put a ring on his finger and sandals on his feet. Bring the fattened calf and kill it. Let's have a feast and celebrate. For this son of mine was dead and is alive again; he was lost and is found.'" So, they began to celebrate.

Challenge: How do you think God feels when we repent and come back to Him? Do you think he is angry, or ready to throw a party in your honor?

Prayer: Abba Father, thank you for treating me with honor even when I have been less than honorable. Thank you for always running towards me as I make my way back to you. Thank you for your unconditional love. Help me to extend that same grace, love, and honor to others. Amen

BLESS THE LORD AT ALL TIMES!

Bless the Lord oh my soul, and all that is within me bless His name! It's easy to praise His name when we are being blessed, and it's very easy to shout His name and proclaim His goodness from the mountaintops, but what about when I'm walking through the valley of the shadow of death, uncertain if the skeletons and dry bones I'm walking amongst will ever live again? Can I find it within my soul to send out a shout of praise, despite the doubt and uncertainty of my circumstance?

The Lord receives our blessings, praises, and prayers as a sweet-smelling aroma, but I'm convinced that a praise sent out and up, despite our doubt and desperate circumstance, is like a sirloin steak vs. spam. Both reach His nostrils but the steak is on a whole other level of holy! Praise Him before the gift, praise Him before the manifestation of the healing, sing out before the saving! At the moment you are drowning, instead of treading water frantically, thrashing trying to save yourself, lift your hands in total surrender, even when the darkness comes, and the only things you see or hear provoke fear, bless His name! This has to be a habit, trained by the fruit of self-discipline. It's easy to bless His name when we feel like it, it's easy to raise our hands with goosebumps on our arms, but what about the times I don't feel anything and everything I see is in opposition to what He said? Will we raise our arms to throw in the towel or bless the Lord at all times?

Love is a choice, not a feeling! When we stop chasing feelings, gird up our loins with truth, and stand firm on what he said, despite what we feel, and when we stay planted in the process and offer praises, we begin to transform into who he called us and set us apart to be. Today, tomorrow, and forevermore, I will bless the Lord at all times!

Psalm 34:1: "I will bless the LORD at all times; his praise shall continually be in my mouth."

Challenge: Do I spend more time complaining or praising? How do I think my life would change for the better if I learned to bless the Lord at all times?

Prayer: Father, I know that the power of life and death are in the tongue. Far too often I find myself complaining instead of praising. I want to be grateful in every circumstance. Help me by the power of your Holy Spirit to govern my words. You deserve my praise in every situation. I bless you, Lord. I give you the highest praise forever and ever. Amen.

THE MIND OF CHRIST

Philippines 2: 5-8: "In your relationships with one another, have the same mindset as Christ Jesus, who, being in very nature God, did not consider equality with God something to be used to His advantage, rather, He made himself nothing by taking the very nature of a servant, being made in human likeness. And being found in appearance as a man, He humbled Himself by becoming obedient to death - even death on a cross!"

As I meditate over this passage, I can't help but feel a deep sense of conviction springing up from the innermost parts of my soul. As I reflect on my past and current relationships, and the way I've lived most of my life, I'm realizing more and more that it looks nothing like a life laid down. I have habitually served my own emotions and have catered to my sense of security. When things got hard, or when I got hurt, I would pull the plug and run. Run back to my vices, escape through new endeavors, or masquerade behind a mask full of indifference, but either way, it was a match to the bridge every time.

Instead of building bridges, I built barricades, and instead of patching up the pavement, I hit it with a wrecking ball and moved on, leaving others to sort through the rubble of my dysfunctional exit. The way of this world always promotes self. Self-preservation, self-promotion, security, and survival. It's far easier to move past people, to move up, than it is to move over to let someone else through. From selfies to spotlights, even serving can become a means of highlighting our efforts.

We are the light of the world. We are not glorious fixtures that stand out to be admired and revered due to our breathtaking ability to shine, but rather a reflection, like the moon is to the sun, continuously illuminating the darkness, as we reflect the glory of Jesus Christ. Our light is not to make a way for ourselves, but to make a way for others. A life laid down is a light that stays on, even if the bills are not paid.

"It is the light in the lantern which shows you the path, not the lantern."

Challenge: What changes do I need to make today so that "my light" is less about illuminating my greatness, and more about lighting up the path for others?

Prayer: You alone are the light that this world so desperately needs. You have filled me with gifts and talents to advance Your kingdom and reflect Your Glory. Illuminate the areas where I have traded Your gifts for self-promotion. Help me use my light to make a way for others instead of glorifying myself. Thank You for the privilege You have given me as a light unto the world. I want to burn bright for you! In Jesus' name, Amen.

A CALLOUSED HEART

I thought I was immovable, and that I had the gift of strength. Nothing ever shook me. My ability to get back up was sheer resilience. I patted myself on the back with pride and judged those around me who had soft hearts. I labeled them as weak and wrote them off, justifying it with a superior spirituality of man-made righteousness. I was not only a fool—I was a fake. I had no strength. My manufactured strength was actually just layers and layers of calloused flesh, and my heart resembled a heel. I was numb—not better than but broken as well as blind. My heart's heel prohibited me from really feeling, and what I thought was my biggest strength became my greatest weakness.

It's no wonder that God's Word couldn't drive me to my knees. I couldn't lift my hands in praise or let out a hallelujah. I couldn't feel the promptings of the Holy Spirit.
My walls were too thick. Years of shame, negative mindsets, and playing the victim had left me hardened, not strong. There's a difference. I judged those who were moved by the Holy Spirit. My animosity to spiritual truths almost sealed my fate.

BUT GOD, who is rich in mercy, pulled out His chainsaw of grace and started sawing away at the layers of my calloused heart. I'm far from free, but at least the majority of my heart is more healed than my heel. I no longer pat myself on the back for a strength I never had, and I continuously ask God to make me aware of my weaknesses. I lift my hands; I kneel and shout! What I used to classify as another's weakness has now become my greatest strength!

Verse: Matthew 13:15 NLT
For the hearts of these people are hardened, and their ears cannot hear, and they have closed their eyes—so their eyes cannot see, and their ears cannot hear, and their hearts cannot understand, and they cannot turn to me and let me heal them.

Challenge: What areas of your heart are still hardened? How do you think that affects your ability to hear, see, and understand the word of God?

Prayer: Father, show me the areas in which my heart is calloused. I give you permission to use your chainsaw. I want to see, hear, and understand correctly. I don't want to live my life in a state of deception. I am open to correction. Soften me by the power of the Holy Spirit. In Jesus' name, Amen.

ANGELS AMONG US

"She is clothed with strength and dignity, and she laughs without any fear of the future" (Proverbs 31:25).

Many people come and go throughout our lives. Some come for a season, some for a specific reason, and then every once in a while, you meet someone who has such an impact that they change your life forever. These are the angels among us. They are God's gift in a person that becomes the present in the moments that change our lives for the better forever.

It's in the kindness of their eyes, the lightness of their laugh, and the magic they bring to everyday, ordinary moments. These are the precious people that make you better just by knowing them. They are confident without being conceited. They have found a way to turn their pain into passion, and that very passion now fuels their purpose. They are life-giving. They are answers on a mission, looking for a problem to solve.

These are people who know they already possess a seat at the table, so, instead of trying to steal your place, they graciously pull out your chair for you. These people use their voices to help you find yours, and in the process, they stand up and speak on your behalf.

This is a rare breed and is almost extinct. When you cross paths with one of these, you know instantly and instinctively that there is something different and special that is beyond what words can express. You will know you are standing among greatness as love radiates and gravitates you in their direction.

"Every good and perfect gift comes from above, coming down from the Father of light" (James 1:17). These angels are God's gift to us. They show us that He loves us so much that He orchestrates their entrance into our lives. They give us hope for a better humanity by proving it is possible to make a difference. They uphold the standard of excellence and compel all of us to want to come up higher. These angels among us are the friends and leaders who give us the courage and motivation to fly.

Challenge: Who in your life, either past or present, did you think of while reading this? How have they motivated and given you the courage to fly? Would anyone say the same about you?

Prayer: Jesus, thank you for the gift of angels among us in the form of friends and leaders. Teach me how to recognize their gifts, presence, and value. Give me the internal motivation to re-gift my experience to others. Amen

BROKEN OR BUSTED?

Am I broken or busted? Am I really sad, sorry, and broken over my sin? Or do I just feel sorry for myself for being busted? There's a big difference between feeling sorry for yourself and being sick and tired of yourself. Until we move from busted to broken, we will never leave the system. It's a sick cycle of I do me, I get caught, I'm sorry I got caught-but I'm not sorry enough to change, so I do me and the cycle repeats. It's a broken system, and until we can look in the mirror, point the finger at ourselves and truly see ourselves for the broken, busted, and disgusting people that we truly are, we have no hope of lasting change.

It's okay to be broken. You can't fix what you won't face, and so some of us need to have a "Come to Jesus" meeting with the monster in the mirror. Deliverance isn't dignified and sometimes our refusal to face who we have become keeps us enslaved within a broken system. If we acknowledge our brokenness, we can be set free. We need to stop seeing broken as being damaged. Instead, it's the starting place for God's grace to begin a new work.

Broken is also the process of being tamed and humbled. You don't break a horse to dispose of it like damaged goods. You break a horse so that the horse can be used. A broken horse isn't worthless because of its brokenness... it's actually worth more. It's the hardest thing in a horse's life that he'll ever have to go through, but it gives him a better, more useful life.

The breaking process is like confronting the monster in the mirror. Confronting this enemy, (aka the inner me), is the beginning of the very process that pulls out our purpose. Broken is working the steps, the steps working you, and finally, the steps working through you. Broken is beautiful, and sorry enough to change. My awareness of my brokenness finally busted me out of the bondage that had chained me to broken systems for years. My only regret - wasting years not looking in the mirror.

Verse: Psalm 51:17
The sacrifices of God are a broken spirit; a broken and contrite heart, O God, You will not despise.

Challenge: When you find yourself caught, do you typically feel broken or just busted? Are you defensive or repentant, and why?

Prayer: Lord, I know sometimes I possess the wild spirit of an untamed horse. I know you're breaking me to build me... Help me submit to your painful yet healing process. Help me to understand what true repentance looks like. Amen.

WHAT TYPE OF LOVE ARE WE GIVING?

As I look over my trainwreck of a past and reflect on the countless times I've loved and lost and tried and lost again, I'm beginning to notice patterns of behavior that always end in heartbreak. So often, I would rely on feelings to dictate the direction of my affection, not fully understanding that feelings are one hundred percent conditional and directly linked to another person's behavior. Expectation is exhausting, and when what I give is directly linked to how you make me feel, my love then becomes conditional. This becomes a counterfeit version of love.

This is an extremely hard concept for me to wrap my head around, but until we get this right, every relationship we encounter and engage in will be warped by a standard set by worldly wisdom, and not the immutable standard of the Word! I can't love anybody out of my own resources! It's impossible! I don't have that kind of love to give! I am a flawed and broken individual that is hellbent on leaning on my own understanding. The type of love that this world needs, the type of love that is unshakable and immovable, cannot be manufactured by self. Love is the only force in this world powerful enough to bring about lasting change, but we have to ask ourselves what is it that we are giving.

Real love is completely void of self! Real Love chose prison chains, endured a thorn in the flesh, and ultimately death, to spread the gospel! Real Love laid down its own life so that others could truly live! Real Love is reckless, dirty, and painful! Real Love will meet you in the hell you have chosen to make your bed in and will stand in front of every tomb and grave you have dug for yourself and say, " Come forth!" Real

Love will always touch the lepers, lift the lame to their feet, and sit patiently waiting at the wells of all our bad decisions! We can't continue to give out a counterfeit version of love, and then complain when we find ourselves heartbroken and bitter behind another person's behavior! We have to stop drawing love out of our own accounts and going bankrupt!

The only love we have to give, the only love that will ever make a difference has to flow from a source outside of ourselves! We have to lay down our feelings, lay down our expectations, and lay down our own understanding, so that what we are actually giving isn't just a label, but is love! Real love will stand on the word of God, even when the ground is shaking, and your heart is breaking! Just think of the difference we could make if we ever truly understood what love is, and then by choice, decided to give it away!

1 Corinthians 13: 4-7: Love is patient and kind. Love is not jealous, boastful, proud, or rude. It does not demand its own way. It is not irritable, and it keeps no record of being wronged. It does not rejoice about injustice but rejoices whenever the truth wins out. Love never gives up, never loses faith, is always hopeful, and endures through every circumstance.

Challenge: In what ways have I made my love conditional to another person's behavior? Am I honestly loving others out of my God's love for me, or is my love fueled solely by my feelings?

Prayer: Jesus, thank you for loving me enough to go to the cross. Thank you for showing me the perfect example of what love looks like. Show me the area where I have made my love both contractual and conditional. Teach me how to truly and genuinely love others so that I become an agent of change in the world. In Jesus' name, Amen.

PERMISSION TO PURSUE

Trust in the LORD with all your heart and lean not on your own understanding; in all your ways submit to him, and he will make your paths straight **(Proverbs 3: 5-6).**

My own understanding coupled with an unsubmitted heart has led me down many crooked paths I was never meant to travel. I have endured heartache, disappointments, and rejection, many of which were self-inflicted wounds I never would or should have had to heal from and would have been completely avoidable had I been truly submitted to God.

As I look back over the habitual patterns and decisions that brought about unnecessary pain in my life, the one common missing denominator in EVERY circumstance, was the permission from God to pursue. In my immaturity, impatience, and foolishness, I would make a decision and then somehow expect God to bless it. I was treating God as if He were merely an asset, and a cosigner to my decisions, instead of the Author of my very existence. I have wasted time, tears, and treasure pouring myself into people and places that were never my assignment or intended purpose. I have wasted precious oil, gifts, and seeds, and in return, have reaped a locusl-eaten harvest of dead works, that will ALL burn up because I moved on feelings instead of faith.

Faith, at its foundation, is trust. My own "understanding" is highly motivated by feelings and fleshly appetites, whereas real faith will not make a move without God's permission to first pursue it. Sadly, from personal experience, I have found that faith is being preached and taught as an emotional state of becoming that arouses our flesh and caters to our carnality. It places the outcome of God's demonstration of power and authority back onto us, by means of mustering up the miraculous (as if we even could). This type of "feelings-based faith" is not only inaccurate, but also completely counterfeit, and at its core, demonic. Faith stands and waits more than it ever moves. Faith, in its purest form, is completely void of fleshly feelings. Faith is trust, and trust is formulated and fortified through relationships. Faith, real faith, is cultivated through obedience and discipline. It is trained up, tested, and approved. Feelings will take us places that faith never would. Faith rejoices just as much over a "No," and a closed door as it does an open one, because its confidence is placed in the Author, not the outcome.

When we submit our feelings and our own understanding to God's standards, we create a platform for God's Glory to be manifested in our lives. God's permission to pursue precedes every blessing and movement of the miraculous. Sure, we can choose to exchange a feel-good experience and call it "faith" and beg for God's blessing, or we can trust every experience by faith and become the blessings we were created to be, showcasing His Glory, as our lives become the altar and platform for His power. Faith will not move without permission to pursue!

Proverbs: 3: 5-6 "Trust in the LORD with all your heart and lean not on your own understanding; in all your ways submit to him, and he will make your paths straight."

Challenge: What things and people have I pursued without first asking God's permission? What consequences have I suffered as a result?

Prayer: Father, I want to be inside of Your will for my life. Help me to trust You, instead of trusting in my own understanding. Teach me how to submit my decisions, dreams, and goals to You. I'm tired of paying the price of moving forward, without permission to pursue. Going forward, I will ask You first because I know You want the best for me. In Jesus' name, Amen.

WHY DO WE SETTLE?

My entire life, I have struggled and battled with the demonic spirit of Religion. The spirit that uses the truth in portraying truth, yet only manages to enslave me further into a legalistic and rigid doctrine of demons. This spirit seeks to place us in a seat of judgment using our own understanding and a self-righteous, lofty knowledge of the scriptures, a spirit that kills while masquerading as enlightenment.

When we find ourselves opinionated and pointing fingers externally instead of inwardly, we are dangerously close to being deceived. We must never forget that the continuing confrontation done by Jesus in the scriptures was always to address this condition. Our knowledge of the Word on our best days, when we preach our best messages is still foolishness and highly erred when compared to His Glory. Even with the purest motives and best intentions, we always fall short of His intended purpose and complete awareness of total truth.

So often do I hear professing Christians attacking and disqualifying God's chosen servants by publicly pointing out their erred theologies. News flash: ALL of our theologies are greatly erred. Who are we to throw stones at, or uncover anyone other than ourselves? We have the audacity to wonder why we are not seeing the gospel fulfilled in its entirety and are quick to formulate justifications to excuse the lack of the miraculous using lowering and labeling the gospel to meet our current unmet expectations. We put all the weight on what we see (self) and settle into a counterfeit identity that misrepresents who we claim to believe.

How can we imitate Christ with half-truths formulated through watered-down religion? How can we be so quick to dismiss healing as if it had a time stamp? If God is the same yesterday, today, and forever, that means the change happened on our end, not His. We are so busy debating and dividing over doctrine, that we have lost sight of the great commission. We are first in line to discredit, chasten and condemn, yet find ourselves on the sidelines when it comes to the laying on of hands, putting down our differences, and becoming the unified body of Christ, fighting together on the battlefield. So, what if we don't share the same point of view? Our unified viewpoint is still the same. Jesus! How can we preach the Gospel to a lost world, when we can't even preach it to ourselves? Yes, some preach out of selfish ambition, rivalry, or envy, but their heart condition is none of our business.

We need to take the Apostle Paul's stance as he clearly and adamantly writes his position in **Philippians 1: (15-18):** "What does it matter... nevertheless the gospel is still going forth no matter what their motives, so in this I will rejoice!" Today, let's choose to lay down our labels, drop all our stones and pick up our crosses. Let's lift one another up, instead of tearing each other down. When we see something, let's not only say something, let's do something! PRAY.

May we refuse to blow the wind up the skirt of a fellow believer, but instead choose to provide a covering. And if we must point fingers and throw stones, let's aim only at ourselves. In doing this, we will be positioned for purpose and marked for a movement of God that not only shatters our boxes but also lifts the lid off our expectations. Today, together, let us not settle for anything less than the full Gospel!

Prayer: Lord, help me to be about your business and to mind my own. I repent for uncovering my fellow believers, especially those whose opinions are different from my own. Teach me by the power of the Holy Spirit, to take the stance of the Apostle Paul and to develop a nevertheless mentality. I want to advance your kingdom and not divide it. In Jesus' name.

WHO DO YOU SAY THAT I AM?

We spend a lot of time looking into the biblical mirror of Christianity, asking ourselves important and identifying questions. We probe the pages, both pursuing and lingering over affirmations that point us toward purpose and reassure our positions. A very popular Christian song (one of my favs) chorus line says boldly, "I am who you say that I am. I am chosen, not forsaken; I am who you say I am." We love declaring this boldly as we sing at the top of our lungs, chest out standing just a little bit taller with every word; I know I do! I feel valued, I feel important, and I can rest reassured that I matter to God. I was not an accident but an intentional choice! And we need this type of reassurance, just like a dope fiend needs a hit (literally), and there is nothing wrong with that.

We are free to return to this well of Godly affirmation as many times as we need to get our identity fix, but what if there's a substantially better source? What if we could learn to shift our perspective and expectation of affirmation off ourselves, and back onto the identity and totality of our Maker? What if we ask ourselves the same question Jesus asked His disciples, "Who do you say that I am?" It's not so much in how we can view ourselves, but rather, it's in what capacity we can elevate and cultivate His identity. Who is He to us? Our identity and the way we view ourselves despite His affirmations, at our best, is still tainted and flawed! We live under the curse of humanity and depravity. At our greatest, we still fall short and miss the mark! We can't pull power out of who we are to Him. That type of thinking is still deeply rooted in self-righteousness and works. The power (even the ability to see ourselves correctly), always has to flow from The Source. It's not what he says about us and can do for us that holds the greater value. Greater is

He who is in me, who desires to work in us and through us, not just for us. The Savior, not the saving, the Healer, not the healing, the Giver, and not just the gifts! Our faith, abilities, gifts, and identity can never be found in ourselves. We have to habitually train ourselves and command our souls to look higher and deeper.

What He says about us is very important, has tremendous value, and holds purpose, but what is more important and what always trumps our identity is His! Jesus asked His disciples a very deep and intentional question, "Who do you say that I am?" It's a great question. The question still echoes generations later. "Who do you say that I am?" How we behold Him far outweighs and outlasts how we view ourselves. We are called, but He is King! We have a purpose, but He holds the ultimate position. We are loved, but He is love! Just something to think about!

Matthew 16:15: "But what about you?" Jesus asked, "Who do you say I am?"

Challenge: Imagine Jesus is looking you directly in the eye, asking the same question. "<u>Your Name</u>, Who do you say that I am? How would our lives look different if we continued to shift our focus off ourselves and learn to behold his identity?

Prayer: Jesus, I say that You are my King. Help me to learn from you, so that I can draw my identity from beholding Yours. Let my self-worth be that of an image bearer. In Jesus' name, Amen.

A SEASON OF STRIPPING

"He cuts off every branch in me that bears no fruit, while every branch that does bear fruit he prunes so that it will be even more fruitful" (John 15:2).

Talk about a terrifying verse! I think we tend to read this scripture without fully comprehending the ramifications of what Jesus is actually teaching. I've spent years crying and feeling heartbroken, frustrated over things and situations that didn't turn out the way I'd hoped or expected. I have felt worthless, unloved, and less than, all behind another person's rejection. I didn't realize that their mistreatment of me was ordained by God! He cuts off every branch in me that bears no fruit, meaning, if what I'm tied to is unable to bring Him Glory, then it's only a matter of time before He cuts it off or trims it back. Sanctification is the inheritance of the righteous, and pruning is the evidence of royalty. As beloved sons and daughters of the King, we are prohibited from shaking up with peasants. Glory flows through our veins!!!! We are a chosen generation and a royal priesthood! We have been snatched from our darkness and depravity, and spotlighted for all eternity! We are a city on a hill that cannot be hidden and anything or anyone that gets in our way or dims down our lights will eventually be cut down or removed! This pruning process is not optional! Jesus wasn't just making a suggestion for our lives; He was telling us how it is! When we say "yes" to God, we say "yes" to His standards! We no longer have the luxury of making our own decisions! We can try, but just look at what happened to Jonah when he refused God's plan! Proverbs 16:9 says it best, "In their hearts humans plan their course, but the Lord establishes their steps." We have in a way, signed up to be ghosted, rejected, and betrayed! It doesn't mean that we are less than, worthless or unlovable. In fact, the opposite is true! We are so loved, so worthy and so purposed that God will not stand for anything or anyone that drains us of our heavenly identities. He will shut the door, leave you on read, or strip away everything that picks on your purpose, and that's a promise!

Challenge: Think about a past situation where God used rejection as a form of pruning in your life. How did you feel at that moment? How do you feel about it now?

Prayer: Rejection hurts like hell. I don't always see your pruning as protection and love. Sometimes all I see is my pain. I know from experience that rejection, in the end, produces fruit in my life. Help me to trust you, even when it hurts. I know you want the best for me. I know your ways are not my own. Thank you for your protection through the means of rejection. Thank you for cutting me to heal me.

THE VOICE OF TRUTH

Casting Crowns put out a song many years ago entitled, "The Voice of Truth." The chorus to the song is this:

But the Voice of Truth tells me a different story. The Voice of Truth says, "Do not be afraid!" And the Voice of Truth says, "This is for My glory" Out of all the voices calling out to me I will choose to listen and believe the Voice of Truth...

Many voices are speaking right now in our nation and all over the world that claim they are telling the truth. From the news, social media, political parties, and pulpits, many different versions that claim to be "truth" are being projected and promoted. Fear, panic, division, and chaos are at an all-time high, mass reproducing, as mainstream media continuously pushes an agenda that targets fear-induced conformity.

Have you ever wondered why the news and social media are called news feeds? Whatever you feed grows stronger and stronger, until it becomes a stronghold that then cripples our ability to discern correctly. Truth has a name, Truth is a person, and Truth is unchanging. Truth is; Jesus Christ is the same yesterday today and forever, and although Truth does not change, our understanding of it should. The Bible says that we go from glory to glory, and from things hidden, to them being revealed. What was once truth for me is no longer, as I come into a greater understanding of who He is. People with the same belief in truth as you will never be able to lead you to a higher level of understanding because they have not yet attained it. Truth comes to challenge our doctrine, traditions, and theologies. Truth is the voice that stands opposite the masses beckoning us out of our comfortable boats, and into the UNKNOWN waters where Jesus stands. Truth whispers, "Do not be afraid" in the middle of the storm, and calls us out from among the crowd.

I am learning, daily, from the spiritual believers and overcomers God has hand-picked, placed, and positioned in my life, that the Voice of Truth is not always recognizable to me because my capacity for truth is limited to my own understanding of what truth is. I'm finding out more and more, that I habitually follow my feelings and common sense (worldly wisdom), over actually following THE TRUTH. I cannot obtain the totality of truth based solely on my own understanding. Growing things change, and things require water to grow, and despite our talents, gifts, and anointings, none of us possess the ability or capability to water ourselves.

There are certain truths that God will not give or reveal to us individually but rather will impart that hidden knowledge and wisdom to those in spiritual authority over us. We cannot train ourselves up in truth any more than a baby can change its diapers. Amid this mystery called life, I would challenge all of us to choose to listen and believe the Voice of Truth in the person and totality of Jesus Christ whose testimony IS the Spirit of prophecy. The Voice of Truth still speaks to us through the prophetic anointing given to the Apostles. The question remains, are we choosing to listen and believe?

2 Timothy 3:16-17: "All Scripture is given by inspiration of God, and is profitable for doctrine, for reproof, for correction, for instruction in righteousness, that the man of God may be complete, thoroughly equipped for every good work."

Challenge: Although there are certain truths that God will not reveal to us, He will impart hidden knowledge and wisdom to those in spiritual authority over us. We can't train ourselves up in truth any more than a baby can change its diapers. Amid this mystery called life, I would challenge all of us to choose to listen and believe the Voice of Truth in the person, as well as the totality of Jesus Christ, whose testimony is the spirit of prophecy. Who are the spiritual leaders in my life? Am I submitted to their authority?

Prayer: Lord, show me those you have placed in authority over me. Give me the humility to submit to their leadership and wisdom. I know they can see things that I'm not able to see. Help me to trust in the prophetic anointing over their lives. I want to listen to understand. Remove my pride. In Jesus' name, Amen.

BREATHING TO DEATH

The chorus to one of my favorite Lecrae songs is:

Help me, Lord, because there's no time left; I'm not living, I'm just breathing to death. Your ways are easy, and they lead me to rest; mine are evil and they lead me to death...

Breathe in, breathe out; it's the danger of just existing. Day in, day out, the pattern of autopilot living becomes so comfortable and familiar, that we are no longer driven to engage, and so, we just exist. Sitting. Spinning.

Purpose and passion become numbed down by the repetitious cycle of our daily to-do lists, and things that once aroused our curiosity have since decayed into an apathetic check-marked box. Indifference and complacency feed off these conditions, and if you don't catch it soon enough, and cut it out like mold on cheese, if left alone, it will contaminate the entire system.

Religion lives in moldy cheese! Jesus came to shock the system, cut the mold, and breathe life into what was once dead, not to stand by, as if to be "unoffensive" and watch as we breathe ourselves to death. We are told in the word to stir up the gifts and to fan the flame, which tells me that just existing, or growing spiritually complacent is not a new issue. The enemy has been trying to back us into boxes and shrink us into moldy systems for decades.

To do nothing with the potential and gifts God is giving you is to do something. It's handing over your spiritual car keys to an unlicensed and unauthorized user and allowing him the freedom to drive around in your whip while you just take a nap in the passenger seat. Wake up! Fan the flame! Snatch your authority back. Stop breathing to death and allow the breath of God to jump-start your purpose. We were created for more than moldy cheese!

Verse:
2 Timothy 1:6-7: For this reason, I remind you to fan into flame the gift of God, which is in you through the laying on of my hands. 7. For the Spirit God gave us does not make us timid, but gives us power, love, and self-discipline.

Challenge: Where in your spiritual walk are you breathing to death (just existing)?
How can you fan the flame of purpose?

Prayer: God, I know you have created me for a purpose. I know there are kingdom tasks with my name assigned to them. Show me where I am prone to grow weary. Expose the boxes I have put you in. Holy Spirit - breathe over my life and fan the flame. Jumpstart my heart, in Jesus' name, Amen.

YOU KNOW MY NAME

Long before His breath spoke into existence the light
I was already a thought, predestined for life
Speaking love's purpose long before earth
His words formed the seed leading up to my birth
Crafted and molded the Potter began
Purposely gifting as part of His plan
Designed and destined, made by The King
Delighting over His work He started to sing
Songs of deliverance, songs of a friend
Everlasting to everlasting
Beginning to end...
Anointed and Chosen, Worthy and Free
This is My Royal blood-bought identity!
Whispers of worth, with thoughts outnumbering sand
Nothing can pluck my life from His hand
Forgiven forever, He didn't think twice
Forever the bridegroom calls me His wife!
He did it before, and He'd do it again
Perfect love laying down His life for a friend
With no record of wrongs, or hard feelings kept...
He's lifted my head every time I've wept
No brokenness, barrier, or continuation of sin
Will ever change His mind on whom He lets in
Not guilt or shame nor hiding the truth
Will ever stop His relentless pursuit.

DEAR DAUGHTER,

Long before I laid the foundations of the Earth, I thought about you. You were in my mind before the stars were in the sky. You were in my heart long before the first heartbeat ever existed. Precious are my thoughts towards you. When I think of love, I think of you and smile. I love you with everlasting love. Your concept of love is warped by your circumstances, and your environment limiting your understanding of who I really am. I love you! Nothing you have ever done has tainted or lessened my love for you; as a matter of fact, I knew it all before you did it, and you are still my number one choice. You always have been, and you always will be, Daddy's little girl.

This world and the people in it will lie to you, making you feel unworthy and undeserving of my love. They will make you feel cheap, point out your imperfections and devalue you based on religious self-righteousness. Don't listen to them. Their day of judgment is coming, and don't become like them, once I deliver you from your Egypt, for I have a plan for you. I am the God who sees you. Your ways are not mine, nor are your thoughts. My ways are higher. Where you see a problem, I see great potential; where you feel the most pain, I plan opportunity, and when your inability limits you, I see a chance to let my Glory shine through your weakness. You are a masterpiece, a royal priesthood, created in advance to do many mighty works that magnify my great name. I am the lover of your soul. I am everything you could need and more. I am everything you've desperately been searching for. I am enough.

When you look in the mirror do you see what I see? Your past is just the canvas where I paint your destiny. Your scars are just a roadmap leading to my grace. All I see is perfection when I look at your beautiful face. You are many things to me, and certainly, you are no mistake. I have a name for you, and it is Chosen, righteous and redeemed. You are my beloved and cherished daughter; I delight over you and sing! There is no price that I wouldn't pay just to hold you close. Let my perfect love surround you and wash away your shame and fear; Daddy's here. I have come so that you may have life, and live life to its fullest, unashamedly free and completely aware of my presence. I will not stop, waiver, or ever change my mind in my Relentless Pursuit of your heart. You are priceless, you are perfectly loved, and you still have a purpose. You always have been and always will be my precious darling princess.

Now come, run away with me into the unknown. Step out of your fear and into my faithfulness. Trust that what I have for you far exceeds your wildest expectations, and I will take you places that you could never manage to obtain or sustain on your own. Get dressed, my dear Cinderella, the ball of this life awaits your beautiful becoming. Shine bright like the breathtaking diamond I created you to be!

Challenge: How do I feel after reading this love letter? What parts of these words do I have a hard time believing and why?

Prayer: Lord, thank you for loving me. Thank you for seeing me in a way that only you can. Lord help me to understand how you see me so that in turn, I can see myself as well as others correctly. In Jesus' name, Amen.

JUST FOR TODAY

Today, my life is redeemed from destruction. I rebuke the devourer off of my life and everything, and person my life is connected to. Today, I stand boldly with my head held high and shoulders back because God alone fights for me. Today, I choose joy, peace, and power. I refuse to settle for an anxious mindset, or anything less than God has in store for me. Today, I refuse offense, choose to forgive, and willingly walk in the good works He has prepared for me in advance. Today, I choose self-control because I am led by the power of the Holy Spirit. I can do all things through Christ who gives me strength.

Today, I choose to shake shame and drop grief like a bad habit in order to free my hands and mind for His purpose. Today, I will make room for His presence. Today, it's not about what I can do, or what He can do for me, but it's about the revelation of what's already been done. Today, I will choose to forgive because I am already forgiven. Today, I will choose to love because love already chose first. Today, I choose to let go so that I have the capacity to pick up and hold unto something far greater. Today, I choose to think before I speak. Today, I will grow my strengths and acknowledge my weaknesses. Today was never promised, so I will cherish it as a gift. If today is all I have left, then today I will choose to live. Today, I will be present and intentional. Today, my actions will reflect my beliefs, and I will let my actions speak for themselves. Today, I will be the friend I so often look for in another.

Today, I will refuse to play the role of judge and I will listen to understand. Today, I raise my standards and lower my need for control. Today, I choose to believe that I am enough because You are enough. Father, just for today, I pray. 🙏